G000300676

IT'S ALL
IN THE BOOK

IT'S ALL
IN THE BOOK

Al Read

W.H. ALLEN · LONDON
1985

Typeset in Palatino by
Phoenix Photosetting, Chatham
Printed and bound in Great Britain by
Mackays of Chatham Ltd, Kent
for the Publishers, W.H. Allen & Co. PLC
44 Hill Street, London W1X 8LB

ISBN 0 491 03590 X

To my 'ghost', Robin Cross – I had to tell somebody the story of my life and he was the only fellow who would listen.

CONTENTS

Introduction: The Mystery of the Missing Tapes   9
1   Experientia Docet   15
2   'Five Minutes and You're on After the Jugglers'   33
3   Grasping the Shadow   53
4   The Price of Fame   105
5   Don't Fight the Monster   123
6   Elizabeth   141
Index   157

INTRODUCTION

The Mystery of the Missing Tapes

INTRODUCTION

The Mystery of the Missing Tapes

I was in the bath in my Yorkshire home when the phone rang. My wife Elizabeth answered it and called up the stairs, 'Darling, it's the BBC in London.'

'The BBC – what the heck can they want?'

Well, time, tide and Auntie Beeb wait for no man. Leaving a soapy trail on the landing carpet, I padded off to answer the call.

'Hello, is that *El*?' said a distant voice in the plummy tones born and bred for the British Broadcasting Corporation.

'Who?' I replied.

'*El*,' said the man from the BBC.

'Is it 'ell,' I said, 'it's *Al*.'

'That's right, El Read. When are you coming down to London? I'd very much like to entertain you both to lunch.'

[11]

'Hm,' I thought, my north country instincts asserting themselves, 'when they ask you to lunch there's usually something behind it.'

In London the red carpet was rolled out for us, and we were ushered in to see the Head of Light Entertainment, Bobby Jaye. Luncheon had been laid on in a plush executive suite. It was very intimate – just the three of us. Bobby was most attentive, but he looked a little uneasy. As we settled down over a glass of sherry, he said, 'There's something important that I must tell you, but I'm not quite sure how to put it.'

'Try,' I said.

'Well . . .' there was long pause filled with much fluttering of nervous hands, 'I really don't know how it happened. It was certainly nothing to do with me – I wasn't here at the time. But we haven't got a single Al Read show in the archives.'

'None?'

'Nothing from 1950 to 1976. Someone seems to have wiped all the tapes. A terrible accident. So we wondered whether you could re-record some of the classics – 'The Decorator', 'The Football Match', 'The Gardener', for example. Let's face it, radio without Read is just not on.'

'May I have another sherry,' I asked. This, at least, would give me a little time to think. It was a serious situation, more than serious. President Nixon would doubtless have been delighted to learn that all of *his* tapes had been consigned to oblivion. I was flabbergasted that this was precisely what had happened to mine. There was one small mercy. All the material was still as alive in my head as the day I wrote it, and all the old scripts were stored safe and sound in my Yorkshire cottage.

Over lunch I made a tentative agreement to re-record some of my shows. I returned home to Yorkshire and, as

I gazed at the piles of old scripts, I decided not merely to preserve the record but to add to it by writing a book – an autobiography. I didn't have the slightest idea how to set about the task and I sought some advice from the journalist Michael Watts. After a pleasant lunch, during which I had told him of the tapes disaster, I had a question for him.

'By the way, Michael, what exactly are "archives"?'

'Old relics,' he replied with a dry laugh.

CHAPTER 1

Experientia Docet

CHAPTER 1

Experientia Docet

I was born in a two up, two down in Kipling Street, Salford, the second of six children. One of my earliest memories is the clump of heavy pit boots and the clatter of clogs on the cobbles as people hurried to work in the early morning.

The writer Walter Greenwood described a community just like Kipling Street in his best-selling novel *Love on the Dole*. Poverty – though we never called it that – was a way of life, something to be coped with. Everybody was in the same boat. It was a close-knit place full of sights and sounds which have disappeared today: travelling knife grinders; the knockers-up, who woke people at the crack of dawn by rapping on their bedroom windows with a long pole; the coalmen, pitch black in their grime and creaking away in their leather harness, filling me as a small lad with a mixture of fascination and terror; the corner shop, sawdust on the floor, with its big casks of butter waiting to be carved up on cool white porcelain slabs. There was always a big red Berkel machine thrumming away as it sliced the bacon. I can picture it as if it was yesterday – my little head barely reaching up to the counter as I caught the whispers of penny-pinching housewives slipping in to buy a couple of slices of corned beef, 'Just for the cat, you know.'

At home in the wintertime we were warmed by the big black-leaded range in the kitchen. In the scullery was the only washing machine of those days – a metal bin in which the laundry was churned around by a wooden shaft fitted with three big wooden pegs. Muscle power not micro chips was the order of the day. In the corner of the scullery stood a red mangle. It took two Read children, clinging on like grim death, to move the big wheel around. The reward for our washday efforts was often some bread and dripping – deliciously jellied underneath where the dripping had set – sprinkled with salt and pepper.

Outside our house lay an exciting world, the life of the street. The small, undramatic details of this way of life have been lovingly recorded by the artist Alan Lowndes, who grew up with me in Salford: lines of dustbins in the back alleys which ran between the rows of houses; a cat basking in the sun; the local fish and chip shop. In those days my mother would send me off to the 'chippie' clutching a basin to be piled high with steaming rock salmon and chips:

'We'll not be a minute, love – we're waiting for chips. Anybody else want peas? Give me your basin, love, thank you. You do know it's cracked at the bottom. Watch what you're doing with that vinegar

[18]

bottle! Look at him – he's squirting it anywhere but on his chips. Come landing in here when they've had a few drinks – I'll stop serving them altogether. TOMMY, WE'RE RUNNING OUT OF FISH. WILL YOU BATTER SOME? I've asked him to cut up some newspapers and he's sat there reading 'em! Are you next, love? You what? Seven of chips, three of fish and four of peas. Now are you sure? It's not seven of fish, three of peas and four of chips? Only last night I gave her four of fish, three of chips and seven of peas and she sent 'em back and said she asked for four of fish, seven of chips and five of peas. Only they're no use to us when they're cold. See – that salt's a bit damp. You'll have to bang it. Won't be long – just waiting for the chips. How's your Glynis? Is she? Has she not? Are these your gloves on the counter? Only that's where he does the fish and I wouldn't like him to come in and batter one. TOMMY – HOW LONG ARE YOU GOING TO BE WITH THOSE POTATOES? What's he doing in that kitchen? Well, would you believe it – he's cooking himself some chips?'

I can also remember where I first heard the 'You'll be lucky' catch phrase. It was at the Old Trafford turnstiles on a Saturday afternoon. There was a tremendous crowd and there were two fellows in front of me, squashed against each other. One says to the other:

'You're not tryin' to get in, are you?'

'Yes I am,' replies the other.

'You'll be lucky, I say you'll be lucky. We've been here half an hour and we're tryin' to get out!'

My own small contribution has been to keep these scenes alive in my comedy. Even as a lad my built-in scanner was busily working away, absorbing the warm, cluttered life around me – housewives gossiping over the garden fence, their husbands yarning away on the street corner as they waited for the pub to open – and storing it away for future use. It was an unconscious process, but the snapshots filed away in my mind were to provide the basis of my comedy, which can be summed up in the simple phrase 'pictures from life'.

There was plenty of opportunity to observe life, as in those days so much of a child's time was spent playing out of doors. There was no television or computer games to while away the hours. I remember making a football out of brown paper tied up with string. Gas street lamps marked the goal posts. There were all kinds of games. Marbles, which we called pin-stoney, was one of them. All you needed was a cardboard box with three small openings in the sides and one on the top. Then you would throw a stoney in at the top and try to get it out of one of the other holes. There was another, less innocent, game we played on dark nights. We would tie a stone to a cotton string, pin it in a window frame and take the end of the string across the street, where we would jerk on the cotton so that the stone kept tapping on the window. When the people came out to see who it was, we had to leg it to avoid a clip over the ear.

Every morning my mother packed me off, neat and scrubbed squeaky clean, to St John's Infants School. Discipline was tough – if you got a bit above yourself a flat-handed cuff across the back of the head was swiftly on its way from teacher. Many of the children at St John's had ragged clothes and heads shaved for ringworm. They were a pathetic sight. It was a penny tram ride to the school, a satisfyingly dramatic journey for a small child. The tramcar rocked and clanked, rang its bell and sent sparks flashing from its huge wheels whenever they crushed a stone on the tramlines. Overhead, small blue flashes sprang from the point where the pick-up drew electricity from the overhead wires. As children we heard terrible stories of cyclists whose wheels had been trapped in the tramlines, whirling them along to a death by crushing from an oncoming or pursuing tram. I don't suppose it ever happened, but it was a suitably cautionary tale.

When I came into the world the Read family was suffering a temporary eclipse in its fortunes. For many years the Read brothers – my father and his brothers Ted and George – had been in the processed meat business. My grandfather had been the first man in Britain to pack meat in tins. In the years leading up to the First World War the firm had prospered under the expert eye of a naturalized German called Alport, who supervised the Read canning operations. Then disaster struck in the form of one Hedley Vickers, a rival butcher and a villain who might have stepped out of the pages of a Victorian 'penny dreadful' novel.

When war broke out in 1914 anyone who produced food became an extremely important person, and Hedley Vickers was determined to be the first man in the queue for the government contracts which were to be handed out. He made Alport an offer he couldn't refuse, including an annual holiday – something unheard of in those days. The wretched Alport dithered, wavered, agonized, and then signed up with the triumphant Hedley Vickers. Now the Read brothers were left with a canning plant, but no supervisor. Out went the meat and back it came in lorryloads. There was a great wailing and gnashing of teeth in the Read plant as the contaminated meat was shovelled into the incinerator.

Vickers swaggered off to buy a Rolls Royce. Its vivid black and yellow colours only seemed to add insult to injury. Puffing on a big cigar and squeezed into a Vicuna

[21]

overcoat complete with a rose in the button-hole, he drove down to London. He was a living example of the old motto, 'You must either be rich or *seem* to be rich.' In London the War Office granted him a contract for bully beef and the vital tin plate licence to can it. In addition, he obtained the backing to set up a factory. As a young man I used to seethe with anger every time I went past the Vickers canning plant.

Vickers went from strength to strength, setting himself up in a big house in the best part of town and sending his sons – Gilbert and Lawrence – to public school. They became the enemy, the posh folks who lived up the hill. The Read brothers were down but not yet out. As my father used to say, 'You're only defeated if you think you are.'

The firm had gone bankrupt for £70,000. My father and mother moved into Kipling Street. While the Read brothers clawed their way back into solvency, my father struggled to make ends meet on an allowance of £2–15/- a week. At least we did not go short of sausages – I some-times think I come from a long line of them. By the time I was six most of the debts had been cleared and we left Kipling Street for a house in Sedgely Park. Impressive wrought iron gates guarded the drive. We were moving up in the world again.

The next big crisis came when the Read brothers fell out. Uncle George handled the money. He was a flashy little man and something of a card, the kind of fellow Lancashire people call a 'bit of a swankpot'. Every Friday he carried the week's receipts to the bank in a big leather Gladstone bag, his bowler hat tipped at a rakish angle. Uncle George did himself very nicely, living in a hand-some bungalow at Richmere, where he was looked after by two maids. Gleaming away in his garage was a six-cylinder Maxwell motor car. Inevitably tongues began to wag – he handled the money after all. The seeds of doubt had been sown, and Garrett – a little accounts clerk who spent his days perched on a tall Dickensian stool – was summoned to go through the books. He discovered what my father and Uncle Ted later referred to euphemistically as 'discrepancies'. There was a showdown and the three brothers became two – E. and H. Read. Unabashed, Uncle George set up his own meat business.

By then I was playing my own part in the family firm. It seems that I was never a little boy. I had an early introduction to the slaughterhouse, taken there by my grandfather and not caring very much for the sight of poleaxed cattle. But it was all part of the process of growing up in a hard school. At the age of eight I was spending the school holidays in our Kent Street factory in Broughton, washing brawn tins in a huge vat. Amid the noise, shouted snatches of conversation and belching clouds of steam, I dreamed about becoming a variety performer. Through the steam I could see my name winking away in lights. I had to wait another thirty years before the dreams came true.

At about this time a small fleet of spanking new Ford 'Tin Lizzie' vans replaced the cart horses which had stamped their way through the local streets pulling our delivery drays. Father frequently took me out in his van. As often as not we would encounter Uncle George, driving along in his delivery van and looking as jaunty as ever. Instantly Father's face would cloud over; his foot would slam down on the accelerator and his hand clamp down on the horn. Blaring like a banshee, our van would bucket past the disgraced but unrepentant Uncle George.

On market day Father would often make a rendezvous at the pub with his friend Sam Edmonds, a well-known local confectioner. Father and Sam would disappear inside for what seemed like hours, but the waiting was always made a delight by Sam's kindness. 'Hop into my van, son and help yourself,' he would say as he held the door open for my father, revealing for a second the mysterious, smokey adult world inside the pub. Sam's van was a small boy's dream, an Aladdin's cave of confectionary treasures, as my grubby little hands rummaged around in the custard cream tray.

Journeys in my father's van were usually more bracing. In winter time it was freezing as I sat huddled up in the passenger seat while Father went about his business. One snowy February morning he came back to find his small son whimpering with the cold. His remedy was characteristically brisk. He made me get out and trot through the slush behind the van until, breathless but a great deal warmer, I was allowed to clamber back in alongside him.

Father was something of a 'character', greatly addicted to gambling and a repository of dry Lancastrian wit. Once I overheard a friend boasting to him that he knew of a pub in Liverpool where for a shilling you could 'get a pint of ale, a meat pie, a packet of Woodbines and a woman.' (The last item on the list was a bit puzzling to my infant ears – I could see what you did with the ale, the pie and the Woodbines, but to what use would you put a woman?) There was a pause as my father drew on his pipe, then, 'Couldn't have been much meat in that pie.'

Father was an expert performer in the local trotting races and demon competitor on the bowls green, where he sometimes played for up to a £100 a match, One night, after recording a famous victory, he returned home very late, a little worse for drink and accompanied by some of his cronies. I was hauled out of bed and, eyes still sticky with sleep, was required to give a little song and dance act on the dining room table. If I remember right I entertained my red-faced, swaying audience with, 'I'm a little brown mouse and I live in a house'. Strong arms lifted me down from the table and one of my father's friends slipped half a crown into the pocket of my pyjama jacket. I suppose that it was my first professional performance.

'Experientia Docet' – 'You learn from experience' – was a motto I picked up from a jam jar label rather than the Latin classes at North Manchester Preparatory Grammar, where Father had sent me to acquire 'a little polish'. It was at the Preparatory Grammar that I made my only foray into 'legitimate' theatre, playing Shylock in *The Merchant of Venice*. I went way over the top, giving him a hump back and leer which might well have been put to better use playing Richard III. My budding theatrical career was cut short on my fifteenth birthday. Father eyed me up and down and said, 'You'd better start on the van.'

I was assigned to the Ford driven by Bennett – I never did learn his Christian name. Bennett was a fat, easygoing man, not the world's greatest salesman. As the van rolled on its way to Bolton we passed grocers after grocers which, it seemed, Read Brothers were not supplying with their range of cooked meats. I asked Bennett why we didn't call on them. 'Not worth the bother,' was the reply. Sensing a challenge, I told Bennett to pull up at the next shop. Almost immediately, round the corner and into view came the imposing frontage of Wilkinson's, a big grocer's in Farnworth. I left the smirking Bennett leaning on the wheel as I marched inside the shop. Despite my confident exterior I was extremely nervous – the jangling bell on the door sounded like a fire engine going past. Behind the counter the proprietor was slicing bacon from the Berkel machine. There was no one else in the shop and, instinctively, I realized that I had a captive audience, the first of many. I paused, took a deep breath and then stepped forward to announce myself: 'Good morning, I represent Read's of Great Britain and I have come to supply you with our incomparable range of cooked meats.' The words had tumbled out before I had time to think about them. The Berkel stopped. Then Mr Wilkinson called into the back of the shop. 'Annie, come and see what we've got out here.' I beckoned through the window to Bennett, who stirred himself into action and came through the door bearing a tray of samples as if they were holy relics. Too late to stop now. I pressed on, clearing a space on the counter.

'May I borrow your knife?' I asked, and with a flourish cut a tasty-looking morsel from the brisket of beef and pushed it right under the astonished Mr Wilkinson's nose. His eyes narrowed a bit and he asked, 'How old are you, son?' Proudly I told him that I was all of fifteen years old. He paused, stroking his chin, and then smiling broadly said, 'All right, you win. I'll take some of the brisket.' I had made my first sale.

Flushed with success we drove on to Walker's of Bolton, another grocer's Read's had never supplied. Again my tactics were successful. Throughout these momentous events Bennett maintained a studied silence. For my part the patter came naturally. It was as if I was selling myself along with the brisket, tongue and boiled ham.

Successful business, like comedy, depends on a combination of courage and imagination. Youth, and sheer ignorance, gave me the courage. The second came as I developed my sales talk, telling jokes on my rounds, practising different accents – everything from Geordie to Cockney – and creating thumbnail sketches of the more colourful characters in our neighbourhood. 'Tell us a joke, Alfred,' the shopkeepers would ask as I came through the door. It always broke the ice, helped to sell a small mountain of meat and revealed the teenage Alfred Read as a frustrated performer.

My father had impressed on me the simple truth that the best salesmen were good listeners as well as smart talkers. As I grew up the voracious scanner in my brain, which previously had soaked up everything like blotting paper, now became more finely tuned. I was able to identify and isolate specific types. Later, at home, I would attempt to recreate their accents and their gestures. It was about this time that I encountered one of the characters who played a big part in my radio shows. If you've ever been to a football match you will have met him too – the loudmouth. Whether standing on the terraces or the touchline, he is always the same, the Johnny Know All with the foghorn voice who conducts a one-sided conversation with the players on the pitch and everyone unfortunate enough to be standing around him:

Come on the Reds! Get stuck into 'em.
Nicely! Oh lovely Cunliffe.
Now get it down the middle.
(Groan of disappointment from the crowd)
Well you big nellie! He's no idea!
What's the matter with Darnley?
Does he want a ball of his own?
Come in number seven!
Look at him – fiddling and fumbling about.
Get rid of it man.
Why don't they drop him and play his missus?
Offside! Offside a mile!
Get some glasses ref!
Course it was offside.
Another yard and he'd have been watching from the terraces.

[27]

(Blast from referee's whistle)
I should think so! Oh never! Never! No! No!
Look at that! Get dressed ref!
He's given it to the other side!
He's playing for 'em. Course he is!
Any more of this and we'll need two men to mark
him!
Come on Carter – run about a bit – keep warm!
He's not had the ball for three matches . . .
Sixty thousand quid – two left feet and playing him
inside right!
They couldn't pick buttercups – never mind a football
team!
Oh don't give it to Barrett . . . anybody but him!
Hey Lofty! Stay where you are – we'll move the goal
posts!

Comedy costs nothing if you look around you. There were loudmouths aplenty on the terraces at Old Trafford, where my father used to take me to watch my heroes, Manchester United. After the game we always went across the road to Wardles, a pastry shop which sold delicious steak and kidney pies. Cupping the pie in my left hand and balancing it with my right, I would bite into it as we walked back through the winter gloom to my father's van. The thick brown gravy always seeped through my fingers and on to my coat and scarf: 'No need to tell me about dribbling – it's all down your jersey,' was my mother's inevitable remark as I came through the door.

I often think that it takes a Northerner to appreciate a real pie. Come to think of it, do they make real pies any more? Many years later, long after Wardles had baked its last pastries and closed its doors, I was at Ascot being entertained in a private dining room by the impresario

Jack Hylton. The table was groaning with fresh salmon
and steaming bowls of buttered new potatoes. Amid the
clink of champagne glasses and braying upper class
accents, Jack leaned over to me and said, 'You like a good
pie don't you?' I agreed. 'Well come on then, let's leave
this lot.' With that he got up and I followed him down
through the crowds to a small mobile canteen selling
pork pies. He bought a couple and bit eagerly into one of
them. 'Great, aren't they? Just like the ones I used to eat
when I was a lad,' he beamed, the salmon and champagne temporarily forgotten. Jack was a Bolton man.

Ascot and Jack Hylton were a long way in the future
when as a lad I was taken to Bolton to watch the great
Will Hay perform. Once again I was absorbing the tech-
niques of comedy. Hay was a master technician, but the
most famous character he created – the seedy,
incompetent schoolmaster more ignorant than his pupils
– was firmly grounded in reality and observation. Hay
was unique, but the characters he played were so real
that you left the theatre with the feeling that, somewhere, the schoolmaster actually existed, floundering
through life in his mildewed mortar board and moth-
eaten gown.

Rip-roaring and rumbustious entertainment was to be
had at Blackburn's Theatre Royal, which often presented
Victorian melodramas of the type everyone still associates with Tod Slaughter, the last of the great 'ham'
actors. The flimsy scenery shook and quivered during
the most exciting scenes. Special effects like snow (there
was always snow) were provided by intermittent
cascades of rice which bounced off the stage like small
hailstones, sometimes drowning the dialogue. Audience
participation was not encouraged, but in these circum-
stances it was inevitable. I well remember one particularly dire production, set in bleak midwinter and almost

drowned in rice. The wretched heroine, cast out of her home and nursing a pathetic bundle in her arms, spent the entire first act wailing that things would be all right 'if only Jack were here.' As soon as the curtain went up on the second act, a burly figure with bristling sideburns, a sailor's cap and a reefer jacket strode purposefully on to the stage. Before he had a chance to remove the clay pipe from his mouth a woman in the gallery had leapt to her feet and bawled across the theatre, 'And a pretty bastard you are, now you have come!'

There are times when some inspired barracking from the audience can be funnier than anything happening on the stage. I recall sitting in the stalls of the Kilburn Empire one wet afternoon watching what must have been the worst talent contest of all time. After a succession of acts and solo turns of varying degrees of dreadfulness, a weird scruffy figure in a dripping ankle-length mackintosh shuffled on to the stage. Stamping his foot with a 'One, two, a one two three', he broke into a cracked, unaccompanied version of 'I'm Looking for an Angel'. He never got beyond the first line. A fearsome-looking woman in the row behind me jumped up and yelled, 'It's about time you looked for some bloody work!' It must have been his wife. The poor man deserved first prize for sheer bravery, at the very least.

There's an old Northern saying that 'Where there's muck there's brass.' The same could be said of steam and fat. The business was prospering and at the age of 23 I was made a director. Soon I was putting my flair for publicity to good effect. When we bought a new fleet of vans, I decided to make the most of it, lining them up for a photograph outside the entrance to a big power station. It looked as if E. and H. Read had also acquired the biggest sausage factory in the world. Business also enabled me to find an outlet for the impulse to perform which kept bubbling up inside me. One day I received an invitation from the chairman of the Grocer's Society to attend their annual dinner dance. I turned up spick and span in my hired Burton's dinner jacket, carrying a small cardboard attaché case containing a scarf, cloth cap and clip-on moustache. After the dinner I was to provide a little entertainment. During the meal I could barely contain myself. 'I do a turn you know', I told the man sitting next to me with all the eager innocence of the amateur entertainer. After the speeches and toasts my moment arrived. It was a blind plunge – like the first time a parachutist steps out of the aeroplane or a diver launches himself into space from the highest board. I set out my case and began carefully to take out my props. Inevitably the audience was consumed with curiosity. The murmur of after-dinner conversation fell away. Mustn't let my hands shake and show just how nervous I am. With scarf, cap and moustache securely in place I started my turn. Alas, it was not original – a rendition of Stanley Holloway's famous monologue 'Albert and the Lion'. I lacked Holloway's precision, so I made up for it with a great deal of enthusiasm. It did the trick, and in a happy daze I sat down to a burst of applause. My neighbour gave me particularly hearty congratulations, and a week later we were supplying all his shops with cooked meats.

Another monologue led to my first marriage. I was in my 'plus fours' period at the time, playing rugger for the Flixton B team and adorning the local golf course in a pair of powder blue creations of the type later made famous by such larger than life professionals as Max Faulkner and Doug Sanders. One day I was playing a round at Farnworth with Alfred Clarke, the manager of the Empress Hall. At the nineteenth hole Clarke suggested that I tell the assembled company a few jokes. Among those who gathered round was the club captain

Fred Entwhistle and his daughter Joyce, a plumply attractive young woman. After a few jokes Joyce's father asked for a monologue. By the time I had finished I had decided to marry his daughter.

Joyce was a pillar of the local operatic society and at the wedding reception both bride and groom did a turn for their relatives and friends. Then we drove off in the fog for a one-day honeymoon in Scarborough – there were no 'winter breaks' in Sardinia or Tunisia in those days. Marriage now introduced me to the relationship which has probably provided more jokes over the centuries than any other, that of man and wife. Wives and comedy are inextricably linked – one only has to think of *The Merry Wives of Windsor*, *The Taming of the Shrew*, Myrna Loy and William Powell in the *Thin Man* films, of George Burns and Gracie Allen. It's the wife's disembodied voice, floating out from the kitchen, which usually brings the daydreaming husband down to earth. I was no exception, and both Joyce and my second wife Elizabeth have been my keenest critics: 'Darling, it's very nice, but it's the second line I don't quite understand.' They are a hard audience to please – just a notch higher on the laughter scale than a wet September matinee at Great Yarmouth.

Her Majesty Queen Elizabeth and Her Royal Highness Princess Margaret meeting the cast of 'For Your Pleasure', a Royal Command Performance, 1953. Al can be seen in the centre background.

BRIGHTEN UP

(BY ORDER OF B.M.A.)

by GILES

WAITING ROOM

"Mrs. Evans tells me that *her* doctor's got an Al Read show to brighten *his* surgery."

London Express Service

Al's fame in 1954 was sufficient to make him the subject of this Giles cartoon.

The finale of the Royal Variety Performance at the London Palladium, 1 November 1954. Al is in the front row, fifth from the right.

Jack Hylton (left) introduces Al to Her Majesty The Queen Mother at the Royal Variety Performance at the London Palladium, 1954.

ADELPHI THEATRE STRAND W.C.2 TEM. 7611

JACK HYLTON and GEORGE & ALFRED BLACK

present

AL READ

in a NEW glamorous Laughter Revue!

'Such is Life'

RIGHT MONKEY

6¹

PROGRAMME

Al's show, 'Such Is Life', opened at the Adelphi Theatre in London in October 1956 and ran for twelve months.

On stage in 'Such Is Life', Al is introducing the well-loved actress, Ada Reeve.

'You'll Be Lucky', one of Al's first horses, and the dam that produced some of his other winners, 'Al Be Lucky', 'You'll Be Lucky Two' and 'Alreado'.

'Messrs Al Read', by the cartoonist, David Langdon.

CHAPTER 2

'Five Minutes and You're on After the Jugglers'

CHAPTER 2

'Five Minutes and You're on After the Jugglers'

After my marriage to Joyce we moved into a small bungalow in Bland Road, overlooking the Prestwich golf course. Rent was just £1 a week. The demands of the family firm kept my mind on sausages, but my heart still felt the tug of showbusiness. If I could not perform I could at least befriend the stars, many of whom relaxed at my golf club at St Annes when they were playing in Blackpool. Among them was Sid Field whom I met when he was playing the Opera House after his first West End show, the smash hit 'Strike a New Note' at the Prince of Wales Theatre. Field had originally been contracted to a man called William Henshall, who had restricted him to playing the North and the Midlands. It was in the Midlands that he was spotted by the impresario George Black. Henshall seemed to have woven a contractual web around Sid Field, but within an hour of its lapsing George Black had signed him up for a London show and struck box-office gold. Field was an overnight sensation and in no time at all he was posing for a portrait by the distinguished artist Dame Laura Knight.

One day over drinks I suggested to Sid a little routine I had dreamed up – 'the artist sketch' – which revolved around a painter whose completion of a new master-piece was constantly interrupted by the pestering atten-tions of a small child. I thought that Jimmy Clitheroe would be perfect as the child but, alas, his agent would not release him and the part went to Pauline Black. At the beginning of the war I gave Sid the idea for another sketch – 'News at Dictation Speed' – which was prompted by the slow, deliberate delivery of the news-readers of the time.

With the coming of the war we found ourselves in the same position which the Read brothers had so badly mishandled in 1914. With the inevitable wartime shortages just around the corner, commodities like meat would have to be 'stretched' in every conceivable way. Sausages were the simple answer, but the demand plunged us into a maelstrom of work. This time I was determined not to miss out on the service contracts which had provided the foundation of the dastardly Hedley Vickers' fortunes. I planned my campaign as carefully as any military operation. First came the reconnaissance. For several days I observed the movements of the NAAFI's northern buyer, who was based in Liverpool. I felt a bit like Sam Spade in 'The Maltese Falcon'. Every day the buyer lunched well – if none too wisely – at the Adelphi Hotel. He always arrived back in his office at 3pm precisely. Having laid my plans I made my move, arriving unannounced in his office shortly after his return from a convivial three hour lunch. As usual I had provided myself with a 'gimmick' – a natty custom-made leather gas mask case filled to the brim with my samples. Ushered into his inner sanctum, I placed the case on the edge of the buyer's desk. He was hypnotized by it. It was a repeat of my 'business' with the cardboard attaché case at the Grocers' dinner. With great deliberation I slowly cleared the desk, just as I had done years before in Mr Wilkinson's shop. Then I brought out the samples one by one.

'Do you make luncheon sausage?' the buyer suddenly asked. Before the war this had been known as 'German sausage' but, for obvious reasons, the name had been changed.

'Of course we make luncheon sausage.'

'Can you produce two tons a week?'

I paused before delivering the *coup de grâce*, 'Oh, is that all?' This was a problem which would have to be solved in double quick time as soon as I left the buyer's premises.

I returned to Liverpool cock-a-hoop. Back at the factory my brother Bill was horrified by my success. How on earth could we lay our hands on the staff to produce this luncheon meat mountain? The result was that we all worked round the clock. I drove a two-ton lorry through the night to deliver the meat to camps in the north-west. After one of my trips I stopped off with my pal Roy Ashbrook at a charming old pub in Lowick.

It was June 1940. France had just collapsed and the outlook was bleak. We fell into conversation with two languid naval officers who appeared to be limbering up for auditions as Noel Coward in 'In Which We Serve'. I asked them what they thought about the situation, particularly France's departure from the conflict. 'Oh, it won't make any difference, old boy,' they drawled, 'they've still got to beat the Navy. Anyway, if things get sticky we can always stooge off to Canada.' This was not a particularly comforting thought for a couple of civilians without quick access to a handy warship if the Germans arrived at Dover. Fired with a desire to join up, I asked the officers if there was any chance of joining their ship, the destroyer Hurricane. Later, Roy and I decided to follow up our decision, but I quickly found that I was in what was termed a 'reserved occupation'. Roy did go to sea, but not aboard the Hurricane. He joined the Merchant Marine and served on the Arctic convoys, one of the most hazardous jobs in the war. Ironically, he came through without a scratch while HMS Hurricane was sunk in action.

My contribution to the defence of the realm was channelled in to the Home Guard. I became a member on its formation, when it was still known as the Local Defence Volunteers. Nearly all the stories about 'Dad's Army' and its endearing lack of preparation are true. I remember hearing that in Manchester several rifles used in the Indian Mutiny were obtained from the Zoological Gardens. At the Drury Lane Theatre in London a hunt through the stage properties yielded four dozen rusting Lee Enfields, relics of some long-forgotten tableau or drama. In Essex a 24-man cutlass platoon was formed under the command of a former naval rating. Perhaps the idea was to use their flashing blades to dazzle the pilots of the massed fleets of Stuka dive bombers which were expected almost hourly as the preliminary to invasion. One of the most amusing Home Guard tales concerned a 63-year-old Zulu and retired circus lion tamer who enrolled in a platoon in the coastal district of Glamorgan. When the Germans came, it was hoped that his appearance on the cliffs, dressed in full regalia, would convince the invaders that a serious error in navigation had been made.

Although at the time I was virtually crippled by sciatica, the Prestwich Home Guard offered no objections to my joining up. I had a feeling I would be as much use in repelling the Germans as the Zulu lion tamer. But I set to with a will, patrolling the local golf course for King and Country. My platoon was luckier than those issued with cutlasses or muskets. We were equipped with Canadian Ross rifles, which had arrived swimming in grease in their packing cases. There was only one slight problem. At first we had no bullets. Then Sergeant Hudson issued us with one apiece – whether we were to use them on the Germans or ourselves was not made clear.

I soon became a section leader. Once again my theatrical instincts came to the fore. I wore my forage cap at the jauntiest of angles and tucked a silver-topped swagger stick under my arm. The limp my sciatica gave me added to the military effect – perhaps a wound sustained in some death-or-glory commando raid. Nevertheless, I felt that some of the professionals should come over to show us just how things were done. I had made a number of friends in the sergeants' mess at a nearby base which we were supplying with sausages. They readily agreed to send over a platoon of Lancashire Fusiliers to give a marching display on the golf course. They made a brave sight as they swung across the first fairway towards the club house where we had our headquarters. I was marching alongside, giving the commands. Now, 'left incline' is a particularly tricky order to give. It never seems quite the right moment to utter the command, and I'm afraid I lingered just a little too long. When finally I barked it out, it was too late. In front of the astonished crowd gathered on the club house balcony the entire platoon disappeared into the biggest bunker on the course.

My other small contribution to the war effort was the

development of Frax Fratters, a canned meal in keeping with the 'make do and mend' philosophy of the time. Like all good ideas it was a simple one – fingers of meat in a potato casing, a meal in a tin. It was a huge success, and because of its unusual name it became for a while part of many comedians' patter.

Frax Fratters provided me with a modest kind of fame at second hand. It was after the war that I made my own first, faltering steps into the world of show-business. One day I was enjoying a drink in the bar on the Central Pier, Blackpool, and entertaining some friends with a description of an imaginary visit to the doctor:

> The loudmouth, sitting in the crowded Doctor's waiting room . . .
> 'Have you brought your bed? – you'll need it the way we're going on in here! I say you'll need it the way we're going on in here. Well you can see for yourself . . . all this side . . . up to that lady in the green hat . . . right up to that bus conductor with the black eye – and for your information he hadn't got that when he came in here . . . then you're after that.'

I was improvising as I went along, borrowing a pair of hornrim spectacles to demonstrate the daunting way doctors use them as a prop to intimidate their patients. Imperiously I waved an imaginary stethoscope about. It was all based on my own experience, which in turn I shared with those around me – everyone has been to the doctor and felt at a disadvantage. As the laughter subsided I noticed a fellow listening intently in the corner of the bar. He came over to me and introduced himself as Peter Webster, the man who ran a children's show on the pier. To my amazement he offered me a spot in a 'semi-pro' show he took every week to the Midland Towers holiday camp. I readily agreed.

A week later I drove over to the camp with Peter to be greeted by the resident comic, an aggressive little man called Billy Percy. Clearly he didn't care for the idea of another funny man muscling in on his own small baili-wick, even if he was only an amateur. He turned to Webster, ignoring me completely, and asked, 'What does he do?' as if I was a performing seal. This rather stumped Peter, and there was an embarrassing pause. Percy turned to me and truculently inquired,

'Well, how long does this thing take?'

'About half an hour,' I replied.

'Five minutes, and you're on after the jugglers.'

The way to the stage was through the kitchen, and I remember progressing nervously towards my first engagement through the clouds of steam rising from thousands of gently boiling potatoes – for a moment I was transported back to my days as a nipper, day dreaming over the murky vats in the Kent Street factory. To Percy's chagrin, my 'doctor' routine went down extremely well.

A week later, in the bar on Blackpool's South Pier, the impresario Jack Taylor sidled up to me puffing away on a big cigar, the showman's stock in trade.

'A little bird tells me you've got a funny sketch as a doctor. Would you like to do it for me next Sunday at the Regal Theatre?'

In a state of mild hysteria I broke the news to Joyce. I could already see my name up in lights. A small army of relatives was dragooned into buying tickets for what was to be my triumph. But as the moment to go on drew nearer and nearer my confidence began to drain away as surely as the sand in an eggtimer. Suffice it to say that I died the death. Not a titter. As I stumbled shaking from my dressing room I was stopped by Albert Burden, a marvellous Newcastle comic, who asked me if everything was all right. Obviously his veteran's eye could spot the signs. I blurted that I would never be so foolish as to appear on a stage again. Outside the stage door, in a semi-circle, stood my relatives, their sheepish upturned faces lit by the dim glow of the bulb above the door. Aunty Florrie broke the silence. Stepping forward, she took my hand and said, 'Never mind, luv, you looked nice and neat, any road.'

Twelve years later I met Jack Taylor again, back in Blackpool with my one man show, 'You'll Be Lucky', at the Queen's Theatre. He persuaded me to do a Sunday night concert at the Blackpool Hippodrome. This was against my better judgement as I was aware of the strict Sunday Observance Act which prohibited comedy shows. So, to play it safe, I acquired the services of the resident pianist to play what could be described as incidental music while I delivered my sketch of 'The Decorator', thus turning it into a monologue which was within the law.

I took the further precaution of hiding a tape recorder under the piano in order to record the performance, should it be necessary to prove its content at a later stage.

So I did the show – quite successfully, I might add – and all seemed to have gone without a hitch – until I received a summons to appear in the local Magistrates Court for breach of the Sunday Observance Act!

I engaged, for my defence, a top QC who happened to be a fellow I went to school with. His cross-examination of the principal witness for the prosecution – the policeman who had reported the offence – was a performance nothing short of brilliant:

'May I ask you a serious question?' he started off. 'Are you a comedian?'

'No,' replied the policeman.

'May I ask you, do you know anything about comedy?'

'I only know what I saw and heard.'

'I see,' continued the lawyer. 'But I think it only fair to agree that to judge what represents comedy would be a little out of your province. Did Mr Read use any jokes or what are described as 'gags' in his performance?'

'No,' replied the policeman.

'Did you hear any music?'

'Yes.'

'I don't recall your mentioning that Mr Read had done the whole performance with a piano player to accompany him.'

'I forgot.'

'Do you know what represents the difference between a comedy sequence and a monologue?'

'No.'

'Was Mr Read dressed up in any way – for instance was he wearing a funny wig, big boots or baggy trousers?'

'No.'

'Was he dressed in similar clothes to those he is wearing today?'

'Yes.'

At this point the lawyer produced my tape recording and suggested to the judge that he should hear exactly what the allegedly offensive performance had consisted of. After listening to the recording with no small amount of amusement himself, the judge dismissed the case.

Prosecution appealed, however, and upon appeal to the Lord Chief Justice I was 'laughed out of court' and fined £50!

Thankfully, in my subsequent career there weren't too many moments as disastrous as my first appearance. However, there was Belfast. Many years later, when I was established, I accepted a booking at the Belfast Opera House, graveyard of many an English comic. The show was booked in for a week, and on the first night I came off to the sound of my own footsteps. Someone shouted after me, 'Why don't you tell us a joke, Al?'

'Things are a bit quiet,' I told the manager the next day.

'Wait till we get to Saturday', was his reply, 'you won't hear yourself. They will have had a few and if I were you, I would keep my act as short as possible.'

During the week my old friend Harry Allen, a superb comic juggler, asked me if he could be moved a place or two up the bill. Shamelessly, I seized my chance. I told him,

'You can have the star spot and close the show on Saturday night if you like, Harry.'

By the time Harry was tossed to the wolves in the Saturday second house I was on the night boat back to Liverpool. I never asked him how he went down, and he never asked to close the bill again.

But Belfast was a long way in the future. My horizons were still very modest. Soon after my flop at the Regency, I was approached by Joe Hill, the musical director at the Grand Theatre, Bolton. I knew Joe quite well as his wife Ada was a member of Joyce's operatic society. Joe was in a spot of trouble. He was organizing the entertainment to follow a dinner given by the directors of a big tanning factory. The comedian Frank Randle was in the top spot, but he had let them down – could I step into his shoes, that night?

I didn't think twice. I had been experimenting with a new idea, an impression of Raymond Glendenning.

Glendenning was a beefy, blustering sports commentator whose special charm was that he appeared to know absolutely nothing about the sport on which he was giving the commentary. I resurrected my false moustache, dug up a hairy tweed cap and drove up to Walker's Tannery. I must confess, I did rather a good Glendenning, fruity-voiced and completely confused about the result of a horse race. I gave the whole thing a mildly surreal touch by choosing absurd names for the horses – I was beginning to flesh out my comedy. Joe Hill was sufficiently impressed to ask me if I would like to play a week at the Grand Theatre, where the popular radio entertainers, Ethell Revnell and Gracie West were topping the bill. I had been gingerly wading into the shallows of the showbusiness pool. Now it was time to start swimming.

My name was to be added to the bottom of the bill before it went to press. As a gesture towards concealment I changed the 'a' in Read to an 'i' and added a small piece of bill matter, 'Jest for Fun'.

Now, how to set about transforming myself from sausage manufacturer to variety star? I went down to Booth's scrap yard and purchased for the princely sum of £4–10/- a massive black and grey De Soto Straight Eight saloon, the kind of the thing Al Jolson might have cruised around above in before the war. Then I drove the De Soto down to the nearest branch of Dunn and Co, where I bought a sporty-looking blue Harris tweed cap. The next stop was the theatre, for my first 'band call', the part of rehearsal in which the band runs through each artiste's special music. I sat at the back of the stalls watching the rest of the cast putting their sheet music down by the footlights and running through it with the boys in the orchestra pit. Of course, I didn't have any music. Joe came to my rescue, deciding that the band

[45]

should play me on with 'I Want to Be Happy'. Then I suggested that I should beef up my act with an impression of Maurice Chevalier singing, 'You've Brought a New Kind of Love to Me'. I sang a few bars for the band and they picked it up. 'Right oh, fellas, that's it.'

Later Ethell Revnell said to me, 'I haven't seen you before.' I told her that it was my debut and, warm-hearted cockney that she was, she gave me a great deal of comfort and reassurance. I needed it as I was terrified. I was given a poky little dressing room at the top of the theatre which I shared with Douggie Francis, a magician.

I would like to say that overnight I became the toast of Bolton, but I didn't exactly paralyse them that week. More important, perhaps, I lasted the week out, but when I went home my father asked me, 'Well, son, which is it to be, sausages or showbusiness?' The De Soto went back to Booth's and I went back to the sausage factory.

By now my father had virtually retired and I was running the business. We were doing very well. One of our best lines were OBAX sausages whose trademark I had cunningly lifted from the OXO lettering. The X at the end of OBAX was formed by a little man, arms and legs akimbo. Before the sausages came on to the market we ran a long string of 'teasing' advertisements, with the line 'Who is Mr X?' above the little dancing man. They worked, filling the public with curiosity about the new product. When the sausages appeared they sold – well like hot cakes, if you'll pardon the mixed metaphor. Curiosity fills the order book in business, and in showbusiness it fills the box-office.

Although I had reluctantly returned to the sausage production line, I still could not resist the temptation to indulge in some 'extra-curricular' activities. I 'almost' became a boxing promoter – 'almost' because my bid to challenge Jack Solomons and Harry Levene lasted just one fight – 15 seconds to be more precise. My one and only fighter was Tommy Reddington, a hod carrier from Lollyhurst, a particular rough part of Manchester. He went into his first professional fight as a light heavyweight and went out of it flat on his back, before he had had time to break sweat. I watched him being carried back to the dressing room, as dead to the world as any of the bricks on his hod. Oddly enough he later changed his name to Felton and had quite a successful career.

Writing about Tommy Reddington reminds me of an amusing night I spent in New York in the mid-fifties. I was staying at the Plaza and received a call from a fellow I had been at school with at North Manchester Preparatory. Now he was a Rabbi and it was his first time in the Big Apple. Could I show him around? I had already arranged to go to the boxing at Madison Square Gardens with a hard-bitten, cigar-chomping agent I knew, so I asked the Rabbi if he would like to come along. Needless to say, he had never been to the fights before and was rather overcome by the occasion. The first bout was between a grizzled Polish middleweight, who looked as if he ate nails for breakfast, and a fresh-faced young Mexican kid. Just before the bell rang for the first round the young Mexican crossed himself vigorously.

'What does that mean?' asked the Rabbi.

'Not a thing unless he can fight,' replied my agent friend.

After my brief flirtation with boxing I turned back to showbusiness. If I could not perform, I could perhaps put my business experience to work as an impresario. An impresario needs two things, the first of which is a big cigar and the second a show.

One night I was standing in Ted Ray's dressing room at the Palace Theatre, Manchester, soaking up the activity and excitement of backstage life. Ted was starring in 'Black Velvet', a spectacular revue mounted by George Black, who was justly famous for his lavish productions. Also in the show was a wonderful personality, Noele Gordon, who went on to become famous as Meg Richardson in 'Crossroads'.

Into the dressing room strolled a dapper young man in a dinner jacket who introduced himself as Barry Piddock, the company manager. I asked him a simple but fateful question,

'How's business?'

'Fabulous. We're taking a lot of money at the box office. I predict that every theatre we play will be booked out. By the way, are you interested in becoming an "angel"?'

An 'angel' is someone who puts money into a show. As the conversation continued it became clear that Barry Piddock had decided that I had all the makings of one. By the time Ted Ray had finished his act I had agreed to put on a revue with Barry Piddock. Gripping me warmly by the hand my new business partner enthused, 'With my expertise and your financial backing, how can we possibly fail?'

In no time at all I found just how easy it was to fail when 'Over to You' opened in Chatham, home of the naval dockyards and what was appropriately called a 'floating population'. This time imagination and courage were not going to be enough. The extra ingredient is commonly known as cash, and in this case it was *mine*!

The costumes arrived in six big wicker skips which Piddock had 'picked up cheap' from one of Eddie Reindeer's touring spectaculars. The scenery was a strange mixture – fragments of various pantomimes and a backdrop from a production of 'A Midsummer Night's Dream' which someone had rescued from a garage. But at least the performers were all reliable troupers: a comic called Harry Pringle; the Musical Elliotts, a first-class act; and Phil Jackley, brother of that fine northern comic Nat Jackley. We'd budgeted for six chorus girls, but only five turned up, so Barry Piddock's wife made up the numbers.

All the props and scenery were loaded into a lorry and driven down to the Theatre Royal, Chatham. I sat in the back perched on a swaying pyramid of wicker skips. The fact that the lorry had been hired from a fish merchant did not help, and the smell of cod seemed like a bad omen.

At Chatham tempers quickly became frayed as we tried to fashion all these bits and pieces into a convincing show. A further shock lay in store when I innocently inquired at the box-office, 'What are the advance bookings for the week?'

I was met with a blank stare, 'What advance bookings?' There was a simple explanation, which I discovered when I walked over to scout out the 'opposition' at the Empire. We were competing against the 'Cheekie Chappie' himself, Max Miller. No contest.

I believe I lost about £850 in the first week. But the persuasive Barry Piddock convinced me that the following week would see a complete turnabout as we were appearing at a much better venue, the Grand Theatre, Clapham. Well, he was right. At the end of the week I had pocketed an extravagant £14 profit, so now I was only £836 down. At this point the owner of the Grand Theatre offered to take the whole lot off my hands for £400.

'What, with 10 dates in the provinces still to come,' I told him, 'I'm convinced I will make money out of this show.' Years later I started using the catchphrase 'You'll Be Lucky' in my shows – I wish I'd thought of it then. On

[49]

we ploughed, through what was fast becoming a nightmare.

The tour was my introduction to the fate of all variety artists, those dreadful Sunday-morning train journeys from empty, echoing stations on to the next date to open on Monday. The scene was a showbusiness cliché come to life as we huddled disconsolately on the wicker baskets waiting for yet another late arrival. Ted Ray coined the perfect phrase for those desolate Sunday-morning scenes, 'Nothing but actors and fish.'

The theatrical digs were another new experience. Some were warm, comfortable and friendly. Others were not. One icy morning the landlady, her face fetchingly framed in curlers, shuffled into my frigid bedroom with what she chose to call 'early morning tea'. Peering blearily over the blankets I noticed that her thumb was submerged in the brown fluid.

'Excuse me,' I said 'but you have your thumb in my tea.'

'Oh, that's all right,' she replied, 'it's not hot.'

I had reached breaking point by the time we arrived in Scunthorpe. I caught the first train home to Lytham St Annes. But with four more dates to play I should have realized that escape would not be that easy. Several days later I was woken by a telephone call in the small hours of the morning. I fumbled for the bedside light and saw that it was 3 a.m. Down the line came Barry Piddock's cultivated voice, calm, unflappable, as suave as ever.

'Phil Jackley has shot himself.'

I nearly said, 'I'm thinking of doing the same thing myself.'

It turned out that Phil had not decided to end it all in Scunthorpe. While loading a revolver with blanks for a comedy scene, he had accidentally shot himself, burning his face quite badly. He had been rushed to hospital but, thankfully, was not on the danger list.

Barry Piddock was still talking, 'There's a slight hitch – he's not insured.' That was it. I thanked Barry for ringing me, told him to lay on everything that was possible for Phil Jackley and arranged a meeting at the Midland Hotel, Manchester, for the next day. When we met I gave him the entire show for nothing and rang down the curtain on my career as an impresario. It was not so much a case of 'nil desperandum' as 'if at first you don't succeed, PACK UP'. After 'Over to You' the sausages seemed like old friends.

CHAPTER 3

Grasping the Shadow

CHAPTER 3

Grasping the Shadow

In everybody's life there comes a moment when fate takes a hand. My moment was approaching, but at the time it seemed that I was wedded to the sausage business for once and for all. Just fancy – married to a sausage! As I watched them rolling off the production line I thought, 'Will no one rid me of these endless bangers?'

Meanwhile, the gravitational pull of showbusiness was as strong as ever. I was always bringing variety performers home with me. One night my guests were Jack Short and May Dalziel, veterans of a double act in which Jack played the accordion and May sang along. They had a young son called Jimmy, who today is the popular comedian Jimmy Logan. However, with them that night was their small daughter Annabelle. When we got home she trotted into my wife's bedroom, dabbed some of Joyce's lipstick roughly in the area of her mouth and entertained us with a song. She is still singing today, for little Annabelle grew up to be that marvellous singer and actress Annie Ross.

On another memorable occasion I brought Ted Ray home to meet my parents. On stage Ted had a magnetic personality – he never failed to grab the audience from the moment he walked on. Off stage he was equally amusing. On that day he was at his brightest and breeziest. But after he had gone my father's only comment was 'Where the hell did you get him from?' The magic never worked on my father. He reminded me of the story of the young comic making his debut at Blackpool. Rather full of himself after his first matinée, he approached an old codger in the theatre bar and asked him what he thought of his act.

'I'll tell thee this, son. I've seen 'em all – Dan Leno, George Robey, Sid Field. None of them made me laugh, and neither did you!'

I had a small hand in launching 'Ray's A Laugh', Ted Ray's immensely successful radio show. Ted had told me that the BBC had approached him with the offer of a series. After a lot of thought he had created a character for himself, a wisecracking reporter called 'Sammy the Snoop'. It struck me that this was too elaborate an approach and I suggested a few simple sketches, including a routine which I called 'Buying a Bed'. Ted must have taken my advice because 'Buying a Bed' was the first sketch in the new series, with Kitty Bluett playing Ted's wife.

At about this time I also ran into Jimmy Jewel and Ben Warris. One evening they told me a string of delightful stories, most of which could never have been performed in public. When I told them the sad tale of 'Over to You', they came up with this story. A cross-talk comedy act

were stranded in the Lancashire town of Warrington on
– you've guessed it – Sunday morning. Neither of them
had the fare to get to their next date. Suddenly one of
them had a brainwave. The Manchester Ship Canal ran
right through the town. Perhaps they could hitch a ride
on a barge. In no time at all they found a bargee who
agreed to let them hop aboard.

'I might as well warn you now,' he told them, 'I'm
carrying a load of manure.'

'No problem at all,' replied the entertainers.

At the first lock they came to, the bargee was asked to
declare what he had on board.

'Three tons of manure, and two actors!' he bellowed to
the lock keeper. For another half a dozen locks the two
'actors' endured this routine in polite silence. As the
seventh approached, they decided that they had had
enough. As the barge glided to a halt the straight man
popped his head up from below and shouted – 'Don't
you think it's time we topped the bill for a change?'

Curiously enough, during this period I got the chance
to appear on the infant BBC television service. This was
some time before I made my radio debut. Once again the
bar in the St Annes golf club had been the scene of an
impromptu performance, this time a little 'golf routine' I
had dreamt up while I was playing on the links. Among
those watching was the baritone Ted Andrews, stepfather of Julie Andrews. Andrews was sufficiently
impressed to obtain a television audition for me at the
Lime Grove studios in London. At the last moment I
decided that I could not go through with it. This didn't
exactly endear me to Ted Andrews, but I have a feeling it saved us both quite a bit of embarrassment. My
personal battle with television still lay a long way in the
future.

Shortly afterwards I was again pitched in at the deep

[57]

end when Ben Warris asked me to take part in an informal cabaret the Water Rats were staging after a dinner in the Majestic Hotel, St Annes. I was immensely flattered and excited. I felt that I had been accepted into the fraternity of comedians even though I was not a professional.

The cabaret took the form of a 'cod' pantomime, and I was cast as the 'Fairy Queen!' It was a stag occasion and when I received the script in the post, the first thing I did was to hide it from Joyce. I'm not squeamish, but the Fairy Queen's dialogue was a little out of character, to say the least. There was a further problem. I have always found it virtually impossible to learn other people's words from a script. They disappear inside a black hole in my mind, never to re-emerge. On the night of the cabaret I was slightly less than word perfect – in fact I couldn't remember a single word, even the blue ones. In desperation I wrote cribs for myself on the palms of my hands. The kindest thing I can say about the cabaret is that it was a cheerful shambles. I was about the most shambolic and least cheerful thing in it, reading my lines from my outstretched palms. Somehow, I felt that I had let the side down.

As usual there was always the factory to go back to. Showbusiness shimmered away like a mirage on the horizon, but the sausages were real enough, and we were selling lots of them. Every year I organized a reception in the Queen's Hotel, Manchester, for our big customers. The year 1950 was no exception, and one night in August of that year I found myself gazing at a row of broad, dinner-jacketed backs as the assorted butchers and buyers got stuck into the lavish cold buffet which I had provided. Standing alone, I felt like a gatecrasher at my own party.

How could I get their attention?

The answers was already there, stored away in my subconscious in the form of a simple question which Joyce had asked me a few weeks before, when I came through the door after a hard day at the office: 'What are you going to do about my mother?' The mother-in-law was coming to stay and Joyce wanted me to hire a decorator to give the spare bedroom a lick of paint before the old trout arrived. A simple enough job, you would think, but in our innocence we had failed to spot the complications which, it seemed, were all too apparent to the expert who arrived on our doorstep a few days later. As he explained it, a coat of paint in the spare bedroom was merely the preliminary step in a massive refurbishment of the entire house. Couldn't we see the deplorable condition it was in? We couldn't, but it took a considerable effort of will power to prevent him for moving in with us permanently to save us from the ravages of dry rot, bellying walls and sinking foundations. The experience had provided me with the first of my 'pictures from life'. I would tell my customers about it. After all, they were a captive audience. I cleared my throat and launched myself into the story. Within a few seconds the buffet had been forgotten and the row of backs had become a row of faces. Then the laughter began. In no time at all I had the decorator on my doorstep.

'Ardyado.'
'. . . Er . . . How do you do?'
'I believe you want the house decorating through.'
'Er . . . no . . . not through. It's just a little room at the top. You see, my wife's mother . . .'
'Is this your own house – have you bought it?'
'Er . . . yes.'
'Pity.'
'. . . Is it?'

[59]

'Bad property this. Built on sand, you know. All sinking. The wall's bellying.'

'. . . Pardon?'

'What we call bellying. Out about a foot is that. See what I mean. Stand behind me. Just look over my shoulder. See? All have to come down. Builder's job is that. You see, if we take your wall down, it means your garage has to come with it. Big job.'

'. . . Yes . . . well, it's the room at the top really . . . perhaps we could . . .'

'Same with your floor. See what I mean. You know what you've got here?'

'. . . Er, no . . .'

'Wet rot. Watch what happens when I jump on it. See! Watch it crack! Come and have a crack with me!'

'. . . Er . . . no. Don't want a crack. If we could just go upstairs, you see. It's only a little room, really . .'

'I'll tell you what! Your decorating's bad in this hall! I say your decorating's bad! I don't know who did it for you before, but by gum, they didn't know their job. I say they didn't know their job! They didn't . . . They did not. Have you seen the paintwork?'

'. . . Pardon?'

'Flakin'. Watch what happens when I kick it! Not been bonded 'See what I mean. I'll kick it again!'

'. . . No . . . if we could just *go upstairs* to the room . . .'

'Have you ever had an accident here?'

'Er . . . no.'

'You will have. Rotten right through. Staircase'll have to come down. Joiner's job is that . . .'

I continued in this vein for another five minutes. When I finished, my customers gathered round, slapping me on the back and pumping my hand. Then a duffel-coated figure pushed his way through the throng and grabbed me by the arm.

'Absolutely fabulous,' he shouted above the babble of congratulations, 'never heard anything like it in my life. Would you mind terribly if I spirit you away for a few minutes?' Turning to address the room with well-bred self-confidence, he reassured them, 'Don't worry, I won't keep him for long.'

Gently but firmly I was steered into the hotel bar. The interloper sat down, called a waiter over and ordered two large whiskies. Then he turned to me.

'My name is Barker Andrews and I am a producer with the BBC's Light Entertainment Department. The door to your suite was open and I couldn't help overhearing your routine. I don't suppose you realize this, but you are going to change the potential of comedy, not only in this country but also the world'.

I nearly choked on my whisky, but Barker Andrews was pressing on.

'I decided on the spot that you must appear on Variety Fanfare. How about it?'

I did my best to put Barker Andrews off, but eventually agreed to meet him for lunch the next day at the Midland Hotel. He had caught me with my defences down. As we sat down to our steak and kidney pie I could see that none of Barker Andrew's enthusiasm had abated. He was almost beside himself with excitement. He continued to press me to perform 'The Decorator' on Variety Fanfare and I continued to stonewall. My feet were planted very firmly on the ground and I was still suspicious of the whole thing, in a North Country kind of way. Variety Fanfare was one of the most popular radio shows of the day – hardly the same kind of thing as the Midland Towers holiday camp.

Gradually Barker Andrews wore me down. By the

time the brandy arrived I had committed myself to appearing on Variety Fanfare, which was to be broadcast in the following week. As we talked I made a mental note that I would have to spend the next few days in endless rehearsals with my relatives and friends to ensure that I was word perfect. But Barker Andrews pre-empted me.

'The thing is, Al, we at the BBC like to have everything neat and tidy. We need a script.'

Now it's one thing talking about the funny side of life and quite another trying to get it down on paper. My immediate reaction was, 'No thank you! I've no idea how to set about it. I've never written a radio script before.' But, as Barker Andrews pointed out, the BBC required everything in writing, in case they had to strike out any material that might be on the bluish side – using the 'blue pencil'.

'Don't worry,' Barker Andrews said, 'we'll find a young chap to help you transform "The Decorator" into a regular script.'

I didn't know it at the time, but this was my second enormous stroke of luck within 36 hours. For the young man the BBC produced to help me was Ronnie Taylor, who was to become my collaborator and friend for many years until his tragic early death.

Next day I was introduced to Ronnie Taylor at the BBC studios at Piccadilly, Manchester. He was waiting for me in a small office which was quite empty except for a desk, two chairs and a typewriter. It seemed as if from the moment I came through the door his fingers were poised.

'I'm just here to "pop" your sketch down,' he told me encouragingly. He wound a blank sheet of paper in the typewriter and looked up expectantly. I waded in: 'I came home from the factory, and before I had time to get my boots off I heard the wife's voice from the kitchen,

"What are you going to do about my mother?" '

After a couple of minutes Ronnie interrupted me with his first question. It was to be the first of thousands.

'How do you spell "How do you do"?'

It took us a few minutes to settle this one. Eventually we spelt the decorator's opening words exactly as he pronounced them – more like a vague threat than a friendly greeting. It was our first act of collaboration.

Almost instantly we established a rapport. Ronnie was anticipating me as I continued with the routine. He asked, 'Do you want to say, "I believe you want the house decorating through" or "I believe you want the 'ouse decorating through"?' Then, 'Do you want the startled reply, "Pardon", written in small type on the same line or double-spaced below it?'

At the time it seemed like a rather foolish decision to have to make. But it was not long before I realized its importance. In the course of our first meeting Ronnie and I had laid the foundations of our partnership almost without thinking about it. Ronnie was a perfectionist. Every suggestion he made or query he raised was aimed towards smoothing my delivery at the microphone. He even suggested using colours to overcome the novel problem, for me, of reading from a script; the wife underlined in green; the decorator in red; my own character – apologetic, nervous and put-upon – in yellow; and my 'bridges' – the linking passages in the script – in blue. As you can see, I was already performing in colour!

It was nearly 11 pm when Ronnie and I finished our first session. He suggested that I stay with him and his wife at Swinton, so that we could make an early start in the morning. After a delightful supper prepared by his wife, he told me about himself. Not only was he a co-producer on Variety Fanfare, he was also a performer in his own right, singing with a group called the Kordites. Suddenly he said,

'You know, what you need is your own signature tune. Something with a catch line that everyone will remember.'

He walked over to the piano in the corner of the room and sat down at it, rubbing his hands together just as he had done over the typewriter.

'Hm, let's see. You call your comedy "Pictures from Life". Life – hm – "What a Life" . . . no . . . "It's My Life" . . . I don't think so . . . How about "Such is Life"?'

What followed is the kind of scene you find in every corny Hollywood biopic of a famous composer. The great man sits down at the piano, hums a few bars to himself, strums away on the keys for a minute or two and then, hey presto, a masterpiece emerges. Within five minutes Ronnie had picked out the tune and within another ten we had added the words.

Such is life
Life is what you make it
Show 'em you can take it on the chin –
With a grin
When Mr Gloom comes around don't let him in!
Remember life's that way
To-day you're feeling happy
But tomorrow joy may turn to strife.
But one thing I've found out –
There's nothing you can do about it –
Such is life!

That piece of philosophy became my signature tune and the title of my BBC radio shows and that philosophy still remains with me – and always will.

When we started again the next morning, I temporarily froze. The words scampered away from my grasp. Suddenly it seemed as if the typewriter was standing in the way of my material, undermining the spontaneity which had come so easily from my first 'performance' in Mr Wilkinson's shop. With hindsight I can see that it was a small intimation of the trouble I would have later with the television camera. Ronnie quickly put my fears at rest, but it still took us three more days to complete the script for the 10-minute sketch. At the time it seemed like the hardest work I had ever done. Oddly enough, Ronnie never laughed once, either then or later. We were so much on the same wavelength that laughter was unnecessary. Moreover, writing comedy is no laughing matter, as any scriptwriter will tell you.

At this point Ronnie helped me in another important way. Before the Variety Fanfare broadcast he rang Paul Cave, the showbiz correspondent of the *Daily Herald*, with the details of my forthcoming appearance on the show. As you can imagine I was a journalist's dream, and on the following day the national press was full of headlines like 'Sausage Maker in Comedy Debut'. It was marvellous publicity.

The broadcast went off without a hitch. Thanks to Ronnie's supreme professionalism, every word was as clear as a bell. The script did not carry a single surplus ounce of weight. Economy has always been my watchword, and Ronnie provided the perfect filter for me to achieve this object. I didn't realize it at the time, but I had arrived. Everything had happened so quickly that I had no time to ponder the perils of the microphone before I was stuck in front of it. If I had begun to think about it, I might have given up, or frozen up, before I had begun. But once again a combination of blind courage and complete ignorance had carried me through.

The BBC were delighted with my performance and

[65]

immediately pressed me to do more broadcasts for them. I agreed, providing that they made Ronnie available to help me. My father was less impressed. He dismissed my success on the radio as 'grasping the shadow'. Sausages were more substantial to him. However, Barker Andrews had plans for me which were anything but shadowy. He had worked his way up from being an engineer on the celebrated ITMA show – 'It's That Man Again', starring Tommy Handley. Now he was empire building and thinking big. I was his discovery and he wanted to showcase me in a lavishly produced 'pilot' for a weekly series. The trouble was, he still thought in terms of ITMA. Like Tommy Handley, I was to remain at the centre while all kinds of comedy actors revolved around me, with dialogue 'coming in and out like lightning', as Barker Andrews excitedly told me.

It was difficult to argue against him. Many years later, the American comedian Fred Allen described radio as 'memory lane'. But this was the last golden age of radio, long before the television had taken a vice-like grip on the public imagination. Radio was the place to succeed, and top performers like Arthur Askey and Richard Murdoch were listened to by massive audiences. ITMA itself had been one of the classics. Barker Andrews was the professional and I was still the amateur – how could I convince him that this style of radio comedy was quite inappropriate for me? Although I was the greenest of radio performers, I already had an instinctive grasp of my strengths and my weaknesses.

As Henry Hall said to me later, 'Never let them know how bad you are.' I was soon to become a 'radio star' in the public's eyes, but I never though of myself as a radio performer in the conventional sense. I was just myself – Al Read. As I once told Ronnie, 'I don't perform – I am.'

Under great pressure I yielded to Barker Andrews.

Excellent performers like Pat Hayes were drafted in to the show. Ray Martin's orchestra was lined up to provide the musical numbers. I was already beginning to feel swamped. Ronnie agreed with me, and after a long council of war, I made one condition with the BBC. If the pilot turned out to be a turkey, I would reserve the right to destroy the disc on which it was recorded.

After the recording there was a big reception. It seemed that droves of BBC bigwigs had turned up to meet me. Curiosity filled the bar, but it failed to fill me with satisfaction. Although everyone was most kind, I knew that the show was no good. So did Ken Adam, who was the head of Light Entertainment. The pilot never went out, and later I kept my promise to break the disc. I still possess acetates of all my later shows, but not that one! If it had been broadcast, I'm sure that my career would have blown up on the launching pad.

After the misfiring pilot the BBC agreed to return to the original concept – 'Taking the Lid off Life'. A weekly show was out – I could not spare the time from my business – so we reached an agreement, previously unheard of at Broadcasting House, to record a monthly show which would be broadcast at lunchtime on Sunday, a prime slot in those days.

With Ronnie to help me I found that I had no shortage of ideas. I didn't need to pace my study or stride the golf course to paint new 'pictures from life'. They were already there, waiting patiently to be released. I would sit down with Ronnie and within minutes something new would bubble up to the surface. Ronnie was the perfect sounding board, always bouncing the ideas back at slightly different angles.

All comedians develop their own style, but it's difficult for them to analyse it. Comedy often disintegrates under the stern gaze of the critic. It's just as hard for a natural

[67]

golfer to describe his swing. Robin Cross, who has helped me write this book, suggested to me that my approach to comedy was 'organic', which makes it sound like something you pick up at the garden centre. What he meant was that the comedy was inseparable from the man, they were both of a piece. The comedy had grown up with me and reflected my own personal experience – it was my own personal experience. I never tried to make people laugh, and there were never any 'gags' as such in my routines. I presented my audience with the obvious. In the same breath I threw the weight of the comedy back on them, always using the word 'you' in my bridges: 'When you walk into a doctor's surgery, there's always someone who says, "Have you always been that funny colour?" '

The scripts I wrote with Ronnie were always very spare, with each word weighed carefully for effect. Very often the most important part was what was *not* said. Anyone can go over the top, and plenty of comics do to get their effects, but it takes a certain amount of confidence and judgement to exercise restraint.

There was nothing outlandish in the scripts. All the storylines were culled from the small embarrassments and frustrations of everyday life. Like taking the nipper to have his hair cut:

'Are all those people before us, Dad? Are they, Dad? Eh, Dad? Dad – Are they all before us? Why don't you answer? Oh, look, Dad, there's Mr Jones out of our street, Hello, Mr Jones, where's your other face? Oh yes – he has, Dad. You told me mother he was two-faced yesterday. What are all these magazines on the table for, Dad? Dad, what are they for? Oh, look, Dad, they've all got pictures in of ladies with no clothes on! Why have they got no clothes on? Are they like my mother – have they nothing to go out in? What do you keep telling me to hush for, Dad – I'm only asking a question! Hello, old man . . . is that a beard, or have you got your face on upside down? What's the matter with that gentleman's head, Dad? It's shiny on top. Bald? What's bald, Dad? Dad What *is* bald? Hasn't any hair on? Did it come off? Will mine come off, Dad? I'll be bald then, won't I? Dad, will you still love me when I'm bald? Hey, Dad, have you seen what it says on this notice? Children under seven half price. What did you tell the barber I was six for, when you know very well I'm eight and a half. Hello, Mr Barber. My Dad has a strap like yours. Are you going to hit that gentleman with it? What do you keep kicking me for, Dad? I'm only asking questions. Oh see . . . look what you've gone and done. You've knocked all the marbles out of my hand. There's one rolled under the barber's chair. Shall I get it Mr Barber? Well, I'm only telling you for your own good, because if you slip on my marble while you've got that razor in your and, you might cut that gentleman's ear off. Mr Barber, if you cut that gentleman's ear off . . . can I have it?'

You see, nothing could be simpler.

Another side to my comedy put me into a category all by myself. I seldom dressed up 'in character'. Everything was achieved by suggestion and the minimum of props. One of my favourite routines was based directly on my childhood experience: two middle-aged working-class women gossiping away about the scandals of the street. All the humour was indirect, and the audience was left to draw its own conclusions about what exactly was being discussed. It wasn't too difficult. Gossip is international currency, from Salford to Sydney:

[69]

So 'er . . .
Oh! She says . . . as good as you, she says . . .
anyhow . . .
That was on the . . . Monday . . . Tuesday . . . Thurs-
day . . . *Friday* night . . .
I know because our Annie had gone to the chip shop
and she'd got some . . . some . . .
Oh no . . . before that . . . I should have told you . . .
Then Frank had been round . . . he'd had one or two
. . . I could see that . . .
He says, 'What's all this about our Nellie?'
I never let – Oh . . . he said – I said . . . Oh no –
She jumped up – she said –
'Well somebody's been talking –
and don't crack on you don't know . . .'
I said 'Oh I see, so you knew about it then . . .'
It went home – she went white!
So I said 'So you needn't bother . . .'
She said, 'Oh' she said,
'There was enough of that at our Billy's wedding . . .'
I thought, 'Right Monkey'.

And the innuendoes . . . if anybody snuffed it – talk
about innuendos then:

I'll never forget it . . . I won't . . .
Up and down them stairs . . . same as I was . . .
And him lying flat on his back . . . gasping for
breath . . .
And not one of them lifting a finger . . .
Brewing tea every five minutes . . .
And your Albert painting the mangle in the kit-
chen . . .
And I've not forgiven her yet for taking up that
coconut, when the Doctor said nothing but gruel . . .

[70]

But as my father always said, 'Where there's a will there's a relative . . .

Great sense of humour, my father had. He fooled them all when it came to his turn:

'I, Herbert Henry Read, being of sound mind and body . . . spent it!'

Many people have remarked that the gossip sketch reminds them of the great Norman Evans' sketch 'Over the Garden Wall'. They are wide of the mark. Norman Evans dressed up in grotesque drag for the sketch and performed surrounded by an elaborate set. Moreover, he was always the listener. I was the listener *and* the talker, setting the scene with just a few brushstrokes: some hand movements and the way I altered my stance, like a bulky woman shifting her weight from one bunioned foot to another and adjusting the delicate equilibrium of a generous bustline. The present-day comedian who has inherited Norman Evans' mantle is Les Dawson, whose monstrous grimacing female characters play a big part in his act. Great fun, perhaps, but all a little obvious for me.

From the beginning I recorded my radio shows at the Paris Pullman cinema, Regent Street. The atmosphere was always relaxed, sometimes a little too relaxed. Every recorded show has its regular members of the audience and inevitably there are one or two who laugh just that little bit louder and longer than the rest. They are performers too, in their own modest way. Then there were the whistlers. From time to time they put me off my stroke, particularly as we occasionally succeeded in applying the finishing touches to the script only minutes before we went on. I was often able to turn a fluff to my advantage, sometimes getting a bigger laugh from it

[71]

than the one I might have anticipated from the correct delivery. Thanks to the magic of 'mixing', these were the laughs that stayed in the programme when we went on the air.

All the most popular radio comedy shows of the early 1950s had casts of carefully crafted and well contrasted characters. So did mine, but the difference was that they were all played by one man, Al Read. I even supplied the woofs and growls of the larger dog which loped through so many of my sketches – eat your heart out, Percy Edwards. My experience with the disastrous 'pilot' had taught me to keep my cards close to my chest. But I still made mistakes. An early guest on the show was the singer Donald Peers, whose signature tune was 'By a Babbling Brook'. I had known Donald for years and had played golf with him many times at St Annes.

Peers was a perfectionist, an immaculate and ultra-meticulous performer. At his suggestion Ronnie Taylor had worked up a short bantering exchange between the two of us which was to follow Donald's spot. We read it through together in rehearsal, and at the end there was a pregnant pause. Then Donald said, 'Al's getting all the laughs.' Eager to avoid any ruffled feathers I suggested that we exchange lines so that Donald had all the gags. When we went on the air we died the death. Donald obviously thought that he was the pro while I was still something of an amateur. But, as the man said, the Ark was built by amateurs and the Titanic by professionals.

Although mine was a one-man comedy show, I always had regular guests. The support – and the 'polish' – was provided by some music. At first the musical spot was filled by the double piano act of Rawicz and Landauer, with whom I had appeared on that momentous Variety Fanfare. They were both fine musicians and charming gentlemen. On one memorable occasion I turned up for the show wearing a new suit whose ill-fitting trousers kept threatening to slide down to my knees. From the rear I looked a bit like a bull elephant strolling down to the water hole. Joachim Rawicz came to my aid and lent me his braces just before I went on. To commemorate the event he later presented me with a pair of red braces. When we turned up at the studio he would always ask, with a twinkle in his eye, 'Are you wearing your braces?'

Within the space of a few months I found myself in an extraordinary position. I had become a 'star' without serving the often grinding apprenticeship which had been the lot of most of my showbusiness contemporaries. The catch phrases which I had remembered from the streets of my youth – 'Right monkey' and 'You'll be lucky' – were on everybody's lips. I had acquired a perfect collaborator in the person of Ronnie Taylor and the perfect medium for my comedy with my monthly radio show. My relations with the BBC were always superb. I had no agent and dealt directly with the men at the top. As a businessman who also happened to be a comedian I never felt that I had to make the compromises and concessions which were sometimes forced on performers who had spent their working lives in showbusiness.

My own business, sausages, was both a lifeline and a marvellous source of publicity. Over thirty years later, after my appearance on Michael Parkinson's chat show, a small girl rushed up in the hospitality room and greeted me with, 'Hello, Mr Sausage'. In the early 1950s, however, the 'Mr Sausage' tag did not always go down so well with everybody in the entertainment world. Ronnie once told me that, as co-producer on Variety Fanfare, he often had to audition 'aspiring northern comedians' in the BBC studios in Manchester. Most of them had gained their experience in the working

[73]

men's clubs, where conditions could be pretty brutal for a comic who failed to raise a laugh or two. The club secretary would ring a bell, and that would be that. Anyone brave or stupid enough to outstay his welcome risked a public lynching. On this occasion Ronnie had to audition six comics. In quick succession they stepped up to the microphone and ran through their acts, with varying degrees of success. This particular batch was worse than usual, and at the end of the audition Ronnie had the embarrassing job of giving them the oldest showbiz line of them all – 'Don't call us, we'll call you.' As an encouragement he made some suggestions as to how they might improve their acts with a few new jokes, a speeding up or slowing down of their delivery, the all-important 'timing'. They listened in polite silence until Ronnie had finished. Then one of them, who was old enough to be his father, took a pace forward and in the bluntest way said,

'I've 'eard what you said and all that, but it means nowt. All I know is you've got to have a bloody sausage factory before you can get on to that radio!'

'It takes all sorts to make a world. I'm glad I'm not one of them.' George Bernard Shaw said that. Well, that might have been true of GBS, who was a rum old bird though no mean performer. But I'm glad to say that I *am* one of them. Entertainment is about people, on both sides of the footlights – performers and their audience. There is nothing quite like the surge of adrenalin you feel as you walk out to a packed house in any theatre. When the theatre happens to be the Coliseum in London, and the audience is there for the Daily Mail Radio Awards of 1951, the feeling is extra special. Among the audience were the panel who had adjudicated on the awards, and I had chosen my material extremely carefully. I had decided that it would have to appeal to the millions listening in to the broadcast rather than the 'stuffed shirt' audience, all of them invited and all of them resplendent in full evening dress. I chose two linked routines, 'A Night Out With the Boys' and 'The Morning After the Night Before'. The first was a classic 'loudmouth' sketch, a picture of pub life as it was and always has been in the corner locals of the North.

For the first few minutes the audience listened to the 'pub scene' with what could only be called polite interest. It seemed as if I had been on the stage for hours. I pressed on into 'The Morning After the Night Before'. Still no reaction. Finally I reached the point where the hung – over husband is shouting downstairs to his wife,

'Where's me clean vest and pants?'

'It's time you got some new ones. I just hope you don't get knocked down, that's all!'

Suddenly the laugh came – one of the biggest I ever heard – as the barriers of reserve came crashing down. Under all that evening dress there were underclothes, some of them a bit tatty no doubt. It was the common factor which bound them all together.

Later that night I was presented with my award, a solid silver replica of the BBC radio microphone mounted on a handsome plinth. I drank in the applause before walking off the stage with my trophy. 'All the way from Mr Wilkinson's shop to the London Coliseum.' I thought to myself. My feeling of elation was quickly punctured when I read the inscription on the plinth: 'Al Read – for the most promising comedy show of 1951'. That brought me down to earth with a bump.

A few minutes later a BBC producer came round to my dressing room with his congratulations.

'Well done, Al old man. By the way, we'd like the trophy back in a week or two. It has to go with all the others in a special display case.'

[75]

I thought, 'Bugger 'em. I'm holding it now, and I'm keeping hold of it.'

I took the trophy home and placed it on the mantelpiece, with the offending inscription turned to the wall, and there it has stood to this day. I can now reveal that I hold the record for retaining a BBC award. Thirty-four years on and I've still got the most promising show on radio. All the others were stolen from the display cabinet and never recovered.

Recognition of a quite different kind came shortly afterwards. I was staying in the Charing Cross Hotel at the time and was just catching forty winks on the bed. The telephone rang. Down the line came a distinguished voice, clearly accustomed to command, 'Mr Al Read? My name is Piers Leigh, and I am with the Royal household. I am ringing to enquire if you would be available to perform before His Majesty the King at Windsor.'

For a moment I thought that it was Donald Peers pulling my leg, but the call was real enough. I was one of the performers invited to entertain the Royal Family and their staff at a Christmas concert. Immediately I faced the problem of how to dress for the occasion. Surely a dinner jacket was the correct attire?

I walked around the corner to Moss Bros in Covent Garden. I felt a bit uneasy as I went through the door. It was like going into a dentist's waiting room – I wasn't sure quite what was going to happen next.

'Can I help you, sir?' one of the floorwalkers, a small bespectacled Cockney, had interrupted up reverie.

'Er . . . pardon . . . oh yes, . . . I would like to hire some evening dress.'

'Very well, sir. Hm, 42 chest? 30 leg?'

I was shown into the fitting room and left there with a range of jackets and trousers. None of them fitted.

'Don't worry, sir – we can take them in – let them

down – let them out.' I had the feeling that this was turning into The Decorator Mark 2.

'Well . . . er . . . you see, it's extremely important that I look my best. I'm due to perform before the Royal Family at Windsor Castle.'

I could see from his expression that the floorwalker's instant reaction was, 'We've got a right one 'ere.' Then he looked at me more closely.

'You're somebody aren't you? I know, you're 'im.'

'Who?'

'That comic – Al Read. Go on, say something.'

'What?'

'What you say on the show; *you know.*'

'Right monkey?' I said, feeling a bit of an idiot.

'Yes, that's the one.' Ere, Alf, come on over, it's Al Read. Go on say it again.'

'Right monkey.'

I emerged from Moss Bros clutching a case containing evening dress which fitted like the proverbial glove. Fame has its advantages.

On the day of the show I travelled down to Windsor feeling fairly tense. Following the directions I had been given, I found myself at the bottom of an impressive staircase. Standing at the top was an extremely demure-looking lady in long black dress. I gulped and bowed deeply. As she came down the stairs towards me, I could see she was shaking with laughter.

'Don't you remember me? I'm Margot Winnick – we met at the races. My husband's band is playing here tonight!'

In the dressing room I stared into the mirror, remembering some advice given to me by an old Scottish comic, Peter Sinclair.

'I'll give you a tip, laddie. Just before you go on, look in the mirror long and hard and say to yourself, 'Well, who's better at doing it than I am?" ' The answer came back, 'Yes, but in evening dress?' I hovered over the Moss Bros suitcase, undecided. Then I decided to 'be myself'. I performed before Their Majesties in my lounge suit. I had chosen two routines, 'The Decorator' and 'The Gardener':

They say life is what you make it, but I'm not so sure about that. Life is not always what *you* make it . . . sometimes it's what the wife makes it! Sunday afternoon, reading the papers . . .
'Are you going to mow that lawn or are we having sheep on it?'
And then the Johnny-know-all watching you from over the fence doesn't help . . .
'I say, when you've finished chucking that soil over your shoulder – do you know you're burying your coat . . .'

There was a particular reason behind my choice of 'The Gardener'. The King was a very keen gardener himself. After the show all the performers were presented to the Royal Family I stood at the end of the line, watching them shake hands and exchange a word or two as they moved slowly towards me. When the King came level with Terry Thomas there was an embarrassing moment. George VI was a heavy smoker and, in an attempt to be informal, TT whipped out a silver cigarette case and offered him one. The King moved quickly on. Finally it was my turn.

'You must be quite a keen gardener,' said the King.

'Well, sir, at the moment I don't seem to get enough time to potter about in the garden.'

'My problem exactly,' said the King. A week later I received a letter from Piers Leigh asking if it was possible to provide His Majesty with a recording of 'The Gardener'. I ran off a special acetate, feeling immensely proud that I had become a small part of the royal record collection.

By now I had managed the transition from radio to stage. The man who made it possible was the bandleader and impresario Henry Hall, who had booked me for a 16-week season at the Central Pier, Blackpool. Blackpool! As a kid I had been overwhelmed by my first sight of the Golden Mile. I stood mesmerized by the sight of a huge mechanical clown which rocked backwards and forwards over the crowds, emitting a regular deep mechanical laugh. All around there had been chatter, laughter and excitement. The pop of rifles in the shooting galleries, the exhilarating roar of the funfairs. And sideshow after sideshow. 'Tip the Goalie into the Water' was one of my favourites. Perched painfully on a metal bar over a chilly tank of water was the keeper of a small soccer goal. Behind him the net beckoned invitingly. If you managed to kick the ball past the goalkeeper he disappeared into the tank with a satisfyingly loud splash. As I ran up to hoof the ball I imagined I was one of my heroes from Manchester United. It skewed wildly off my toe and sped into the top of the goal, sending the goalie tumbling into his damp temporary oblivion. Then there was 'Roll the Penny'. For a few agonizing seconds my whole life was bound up with the coin's slow wobbling descent towards the chequerboard of numbers. Would I win the goldfish? I always seemed doomed to disappointment as the barker shouted out, 'Sorry, sonny, it's just on the line.'

And then there were the fortune tellers. They always seemed to do a roaring trade, and I suspect they always will. There is a fatal fascination about 'peeping into the future'. During the run of my first Blackpool show –

[79]

'Right Monkey' – I wandered into a fortune teller's booth on the Golden Mile. Madame Petulengro was her name and the outside of her booth was plastered with photographs of the famous people whose palms she had read. She knew the stars all right, in more senses than one.

Now Madame Petulengro told me something that has influenced me ever since, like a thread running through my life.

'You are Pisces,' she told me 'artistic, a funny man, a comedian. You must always remember the letter P and its importance in your life – you will find that it will be very lucky for you.'

At the time I didn't take much notice of Madame Petulengro's advice, but as the years have gone by I have often paused to think about her words. The Palladium – she told me that I'd play there, and so I did. And there were all the other Ps which came to mind. Perseverance, which took the sausage business through the war and helped me to secure those big NAAFI orders. Publicity and Press, both of which have been very kind to me throughout my career. Presenting People to People – the essence of my comedy. Public speaking, which in a very real sense gave me my start. But I'd better pack up before all these Ps drive me potty!

Now I was back in Blackpool with 'Right Monkey' in lights all the way down the pier and a supporting bill which included David Hughes and the comedian Johnny Brandon.

Very sensibly Henry Hall had given me a week's warm-up in Nottingham. He sprang it on me as a complete surprise. One night he suggested we drive down to Nottingham.

'You'll soon see why', he told me.

As we drove through the night I wondered what was afoot. We passed a signpost,' Nottingham 5 miles'. Then

[80]

I got the shock of my life. Illuminated by the glare of the powerful headlights was a huge hoarding bearing the legend 'AL READ – RIGHT MONKEY'. We got to the theatre at 4 am, the time when spirits are supposed to be at their lowest ebb. It seemed that everywhere I looked I saw my name. It was a sobering sight and I told Henry,

'I hope you know what you're doing.'

Later that day I remembered a conversation I had had with Sid Field during the run of his second London show 'Strike a New Note'. Sid had remarked, 'When I came to the West End, I'd never been nearer to London than Birmingham. I was worried sick. I went straight to the Prince of Wales and walked up and down in front of the darkened theatre. Then I thought "What the hell! What am I worried about? It's only a building." ' I felt the same way in Nottingham.

Henry Hall had pulled a shrewd psychological stroke. Once again I had little or no time to freeze up. The speed at which things happened over-rode my inexperience. However, I had already chosen my stage outfit in readiness for the Blackpool run. The show in Nottingham was sold out in advance, and the principal reason for this was curiosity. People had heard me on the radio. Now they wanted to see what I looked like. I had deliberately capitalized on this by giving no interviews and posing for no photographs. It was a small echo of 'Who is Mr X?' – Who is this guy Read?

Nevertheless I had to ensure that when I walked on stage for the first time, I would confound the audience's expectations. No doubt they anticipated a comedian dressed 'in character' – like the Decorator – in cloth cap and overalls. I had other ideas. I had ordered from my tailor a superbly fitting hacking jacket and grey flannel trousers. It was not The Decorator who strolled on to the stage but the epitome of unostentatious elegance. There were several seconds of silent astonishment as I stood in the spotlight. Then the laughter began.

After the show there was a knock on my dressing room door and in came Harry Allen, a juggler in the show. He was a burly, bowler-hatted man with a rose in his buttonhole. Hanging around Harry there was always a whiff of the great days of music hall.

'Do you play golf?' he asked. 'You do. How about a game tomorrow?' We had a pleasant round the next day on the local golf course, watched by a herd of deer, whose steady ruminative mastication made them look as if they were weighing up each shot. Harry became a great pal and a regular golf partner. Something amusing usually happened on a round with Harry. One day we were playing with Dave Morris, a little comic who was extremely shortsighted. He could hardly see beyond the end of the tee. To overcome his additional handicap, he was always consulting a card which bore the length of each hole. When we reached the long ninth, there was a small explosion from our little friend,

'76,985 yards. I know this hole is meant to be long, but this is ridiculous.'

Harry peered over his shoulder,

'You're looking at a ten bob note!'

At my first summer show in Blackpool I had done little more than repeat my success with 'The Decorator'. Looking back, it seems remarkable that a career could be founded on such a simple thing. Nevertheless, it was not long before I began to expand my repertoire – the demands of the monthly radio show ensured that.

I had complete control over the radio show, but I remained extremely wary of committing myself to perform in situations where the ultimate control lay in other people's hands. In the early days I did not have to think twice about turning down invitations from Val Parnell to appear in Royal Command performances. These events are a double-edged sword; a great honour but something of a risk as well. Everyone remembers the film clip of Lonnie Donegan, in a lather of nerves, completely forgetting the lines of his hit single 'My Old Man's a Dustman'. I shall never forget the sight of Howard Keel – all 6ft 3in of him – literally 'keeling over' with stage fright. Then, as now, the Royal Command Performance received national coverage. On tour you moved from one pocket of the country to another, and this enabled you to repeat your act many times as you went around. In the days of music hall a supporting act could go through a lifetime in showbusiness with just one routine! In addition there is a lot of showbiz politics involved in the organization of the Royal Command Performance, and this can also prove a minefield for the unwary. At this early stage in my development as a performer I was reluctant to expose myself to the kind of 'overkill' which even today can nip a career in the bud. It didn't need much imagination to guess the effect on my box-office of a headline like 'Al Read Flops in Command Performance'. I would have been finished almost before I had started.

Despite my native caution I did not have to wait as long as my old friend Sid Field for my debut in the West End. As so often happens, I got my chance through another's misfortune. Frank Randle was one of the most popular comedians in the North. Slack-jawed, permanently flustered and, on occasion, immensely vulgar, he was a kind of genius in his own way. He dubbed himself 'the master of the single entendre'. He had also become a cinema hit in a cheaply made film of 1940, Somewhere in Camp, a knockabout comedy starring Harry Korris. For the next twelve years Frank turned out a stream of chaotic little farces, made for about a couple of packets of Woodbines, all of them featuring the 'awkward squad' routines for which he was famous. He once asked me to fill a guest spot in one of his films – I think it was 'It's a Grand Life', which featured a busty young Diana Dors. Sensibly, I declined. At the same time Frank was preparing to make his West End debut at the Adelphi Theatre in the Strand. He lasted precisely two weeks. Frank's humour just didn't reach audiences in the South.

Undeterred, the impresario Jack Hylton decided to put another northern comedian into the Adelphi – Al Read. Most of the scenery for the show came down from an Alfred Black revue in Blackpool, plus 26 Tiller girls and 'The Sinking of the Armada', a spectacular tableau which closed the first act. When I set out to drive down to London to meet the press I still wasn't sure who was in the supporting bill. I had been delayed leaving the factory and as a result was about three hours late for the press conference. When I arrived at the Adelphi, there were still a few disconsolate hacks there sampling Jack's hospitality. I was able to turn this unfortunate start to my advantage. Stars are well known for their tantrums or sudden last-minute 'diplomatic illnesses'. This was the first time that a headliner was late for a press conference because of a crisis in his sausage factory.

The journalists who had stayed on had plenty of questions for me, but they kept coming back to the same one.

'We know your radio show, Al, and all the characters in it. But how do you think this type of humour will go down in the south?'

I remember replying, 'The radio audience listen to the show everywhere – north, south and all other points of the compass. If you think you're going to catch me on that one, "You'll Be Lucky"! I'm saying nowt.'

I had left the sausage factory in the hands of my

directors and went into rehearsal for what we hoped would be a long run. In fact it exceeded my wildest expectations – nearly twelve months. By now, of course, something more than 'The Decorator' was required, and I was able to provide it. The 'loudmouth' character had come a long way since the early days, but my basic approach had changed little since the time I first stepped on to the stage at Nottingham in my hacking jacket. Now the hacking jacket had been replaced by a beautifully tailored three-piece suit with gussets stitched into the back of the waistcoat, allowing me to ram my thumbs into the pockets and yank it downwards. When I came on, the first thing the audience saw was this impeccably suited figure, complete with shooting stick and bowler hat. After my introductory patter, I placed the shooting stick on the stage – with the point sticking upwards ready to receive the bowler hat. Then a flat cap and a muffler were tossed up to me from the orchestra pit. On they went and into my pockets went my thumbs. I settled down into a bow-legged, truculent stance and within the space of a few seconds gentlemanly Al Read had become the 'loudmouth'.

'Make 'em wait', Harry Allen had told me years before in Nottingham. It was good advice. I always gave myself the time and space in which to turn the audience's expectations upside down. One of my entrances was made to the swelling tones of 'Granada'. The band were going full tilt. As the music reached its climax I stood quietly by the microphone. 'Granada' came to an end with an enormous crash. Silence. Then I look up and say, 'Aren't carpets dear these days?'

The leap from home and the sausage factory to life in the West End was dramatic. I lived in some style in the Mayfair Hotel, a far cry from the theatrical digs I had endured during the disastrous tour with 'Over to You'.

[85]

In these surroundings I soon encountered the phenom-
enon which I call 'the silken cord'. Everyone who has
been in the entertainment business has experienced the
ambiguous pleasures of the 'silken cord'. It's not as
mysterious as it sounds. Quite simply, it's an agent's or
impresario's way of entangling an artist in a web of
obligations. Like 'the bird in the gilded cage', the pros-
pect may seem fine, if all you want to do is to gaze at the
world through a set of expensive bars. I never had an
agent, but from time to time I had to exhibit some fancy
footwork to dodge the 'silken cord' which was snaking
towards my neck like a cowboy's lasso.

While I was rehearsing for the Adelphi show, I was
invited to a party thrown by an important agent whom I
had met in Blackpool. It was a lavish affair. Champagne
was flowing and half of the top names in showbusiness
were there. My eye was caught by a beautiful young girl
sitting in the corner. She was slim and blonde, with a
classically lovely face. We fell into conversation, as they
say, and talked about the hard life she had endured in
postwar Italy, where girls would sell themselves to GIs
for a packet of cigarettes. She had escaped, fought her
way out of the poverty trap and become a fashion model.
Now she was determined to break into the movie business – later she became a perennial Rank starlet. As I was
leaving, the agent asked me to take her home.

I did. As we drove along in my car she professed
herself to be 'astonished' that I was living in such an
expensive hotel. Didn't I get lonely? Wouldn't I prefer to
stay with her – and her mother – in Bayswater? I declined
her offer, but I did have a drink with her a few days later
at my hotel. It was an early lesson in the 'silken cord' and
how to avoid it.

A calculating agent can sometimes put you into
trouble just so that he can get you out of it. Jack Hylton

was no exception. Arthur Askey was tied to him throughout his career and could never get free. I was always careful to maintain my independence. I well remember one revealing incident which occurred at the end of a nationwide tour in 1957. The show was 'Such is Life' and the New Theatre, Oxford, was our last date before we took the show into the West End. In the show was a young Swedish soubrette, very attractive and gamine with closely cropped hair. After the last performance at Oxford she told me that she was not being retained for the show's West End run. She didn't know why and was clearly very upset. I asked the producer George Black if she could be kept in the show.

'I don't see why not,' he said to me with a broad wink. When the show opened in London I escorted the young woman to the Albany Club, which was then owned by Jack Hylton. After a drink or two we took a twirl around the dance floor. My young partner leaned towards me affectionately and, as she did so, several flash bulbs exploded by my right ear. Next day I confronted Jack Hylton. He leaned back in his chair, puffing on a cigar the size of a small Zeppelin.

'I don't think you're being at all wise having this affair, Al.'

'What affair?' I spluttered.

'Well, I think I ought to tell you this. Her first husband committed suicide. She's bad news. It's for your own good I'm telling you this.' And with that he made a great show of handing back to me the negatives of the photographs taken the night before in the Albany. All for my own protection, you see, and about as subtle as a combine harvester on a suburban lawn.

Jack was a master of the *fait accompli*. Walter Greenwood described it perfectly in one of his plays. A pub scene, and standing at the bar with a well-earned pint is a workman. Next to him a wizened old biddy with a shawl wrapped round her thin old shoulders, a familiar enough sight in the North in the twenties and thirties. The workman drains his pint, orders a fresh one and, while it's being drawn, ambles off to the Gents. When he re-emerges, he just catches a glimpse of the old biddy sneaking a gulp from his freshly poured glass.

'Eh! You've been suppin' my beer!' he said.

'Eeh, I know I've supped it. Should I have done?'

The perfect *fait accompli*.

One day, while I was appearing at the Bristol Hippo-drome, I took a telephone call from Jack in my dressing room.

'Well, how does it feel to be a racehorse owner?'

'What?'

'My daughter Jackie has bought you two yearlings at Newmarket sales.'

Of course, all of this was with my money! Jack hadn't bothered to ask me first, but he had made sure that the press knew. No sooner was he off the phone than I received a string of calls from journalists wanting to know what I was going to call the two horses I had just 'acquired'. Recovering from my shock, I told them, ' "You'll be Lucky" and "Such is Life" '. Thus I was led by the nose into the world of horse-racing. A few more shocks lay in store for me before I found my feet. I don't suppose Gordon Richards or Lester Piggott knew much about what went into a sausage. At the time I was equally ignorant of the behind-the-scenes world of horse racing. I well remember 'You'll be Lucky's' first outing, at Lingfield. Watching her in the parade ring, I asked my trainer Monty Smythe about her chances. His reply was a thumbnail sketch of 'racing talk'.

'Well . . . she's in with a good lot, you know. Ground's not quite to her liking, but if it dries out it will do her no harm. She might be worth an each way bet. Not a lot, though.'

'How much?'

'Oh, no more than a couple of hundred quid!'

While I chewed on this alarming piece of advice I bumped into the jockey who was riding the favourite. He had a quick word with me in the ring.

'Whatever gets past me will win. Put £100 on for me,' he said rather cryptically out of the corner of his mouth before sidling off.

The race was a cracker, with You'll be Lucky squeezing in to win a photo finish from the favourite at 100-8. I was beside myself with excitement. It was only later that I realized that I had forgotten to place the bet for the rival jockey. The next day I met Monty Smythe in London and asked him what I should do about it.

'Oh, don't worry about that,' Monty replied, 'he meant you to put the money on *his* horse!'

It was only after the success of You'll Be Lucky that I accepted an invitation from Val Parnell to appear at the Palladium in a Royal Command Performance. I quickly decided on my sketch – 'The Joys of Motoring' – and on my entrance. I was going to drive on to the stage in a car. The only problem was to find the right car. I arrived back at the Mayfair Hotel still pondering the choice, and there, parked right outside the main entrance, was the answer: an extraordinary looking vehicle, a kind of sports car with an Austin 7 body. I asked the commissionaire if he knew its owner, explaining to him that it would be the perfect car for my spot in the Command Performance.

'No problem, Mr Read, I know the young fellow. I'll send him up to your suite.'

A few minutes later there was a knock on my door. In came a natty young man who looked a bit like the Kenneth More character in the film *Genevieve* – yellow check waistcoat, cavalry twills, gleaming brogues. There was only one difference – he was a bit sharper than the character Ken played.

He let me do all the talking as I ran over my reasons for wanting to borrow his car. After all, I was the one who wanted it so badly, and doubtless the commissionaire had already put him in the picture. He played dumb.

'Would you be prepared to sell it?' I asked finally. We fenced about for a bit.

'What about £100', I enquired. He merely laughed.

'£200?'

'Make it £500.'

Eventually we agreed on £250 and he went away with a cheque in his pocket, no doubt feeling that he had done a good day's work. The Sunday of a Royal Command performance is taken up with rehearsals. The show goes on that night. I took a quick band call and then went back to the hotel to relax before the show. No sooner had I dozed off than I was woken up by the telephone. On the line was Billy Moxon, an old vaudevillian who was now a stage hand at the Palladium. He was fixing up the car backstage for me.

'The car can't go on,' Billy said, 'we're in a helluva mess here.' It turned out that there was no way to get the car off at the end of the act as its exit route was blocked by scenery which had been cleared away from the current show to make room for the Command Performance. Charlie Henry, the producer, had put his foot down and had been backed up by Val Parnell. In the middle of this conversation a telegram arrived from Val Parnell wishing me 'Good Luck for Tonight'. I was going to need it.

As soon as Billy Moxon got off the line I rang Ronnie Taylor, a man who never panicked. He considered the situation for a moment or two and then asked, 'Can Billy lay his hands on a steering wheel and a number plate?'

It turned out that Billy could. I made my entrance

holding the steering wheel and number plate and told the audience that the stage manager had asked me to announce that the owner of XJY 382 should call at the stage door, where he could collect the rest of his car. The remainder of the routine was a belter.

I always seemed to run into problems when I appeared in front of the Royal Family. Several years later Jack Hylton asked me to do a spot in a show at the Palace Theatre, Manchester, which was to be attended by the Queen Mother. At the time he owed me £35,000 and this was, I suspect, his own way of trying to square things up at minimum cost to himself. I was appearing at Blackpool at the time and one of the sketches in the show – 'The Birth of the New Baby', with Jimmy Clitheroe – was bringing the house down. Jack wanted us to perform the sketch in Manchester. I agreed, with one condition. The set for the Blackpool show was very dog-eared after the long run and I felt that it just wouldn't do for a Command Performance. Jack told me that he would send the ubiquitous Johnny Russell up to Manchester to organize a spanking new set. On the day of the show Jimmy and I turned up at the Palace for our band call.

'Has the set come?' I asked Bill Taylor, the theatre manager.

'What set, Al?'

Once again it was panic stations. Jack had never had the slightest intention of giving us a new set. He had merely agreed to send up Johnny Russell as a ploy to keep me sweet. After a few frantic phone calls we had the old set loaded on to a lorry and driven down from Blackpool. Did it make any difference? In the end, not a bit. Jack knew this all along, but for me it was another lesson in the wily ways of impresarios.

It was in this show that I witnessed one of the funniest

pieces of off-the-cuff humour I ever saw. Closing the first half was Albert Modley, a great Northern comic and in private life one of the most modest and unassuming men you could hope to meet. He punctuated his act with a nervous laugh which will always be remembered by those who saw him perform. Throughout the show all the artistes had been performing with one eye cocked at the royal box. Then on shuffled Albert with his back to the Queen Mother. He stood gazing up at the empty box on the opposite side of the theatre.

'Eeh, 'ave they gone?' he asked the audience, 'by 'Eck, they tell you nowt 'ere!'

When I stepped up to the microphone on Variety Fanfare, radio was still king. Television was little more than a cloud on the horizon. In 1950 there were only about 350,000 sets in the country. Ten years later there were about 10 million sets in operation while the sale of TV licences had already well outstripped those for the radio.

It was Roy Thomson who, when talking of the commercial stations, described television as 'a licence to print money'. There was no shortage of entrepreneurs who agreed with him. Jack Hylton was one of them. As television took a hold he had already agreed to supply Rediffusion with a series of variety shows featuring top-line performers like Jack Buchanan, Arthur Askey and Jimmy Edwards. But there was another who was not willing to play ball – Al Read. Jack was flabbergasted when I told him that I was not prepared to appear on the 'pilot' show that he was lining up for Rediffusion.

'I made you,' he blustered

'I think my radio shows made me, Jack,' I replied. Jack tried everything, but I was adamant. No television. Askey and Buchanan were the first sacrificial lambs on the altar of Jack's ambition. The show was a disaster. Jack bulldozed on and soon acquired an important interest in the television station, TWW (Television Wales and the West).

'What's it going to get you?' I asked Jack one day.

'Power,' he replied, bunching his fist and thrusting it under my nose, 'that's what I'll get – power.'

I was taken aback by his vehemence.

'Open your hand, Jack,' I said to him quietly. 'How much power do you think you have there now?' I added, looking down at his empty palm. In a sense Jack was 'grasping at the shadow'.

Jack virtually resorted to blackmail to try to get me on to television. He held up the returns on my 1957 show at the Adelphi – 'Such is Life' – until he owed me about £35,000. I did not go to see him about the money, and when he visited my dressing room after the final performance, I never mentioned it. This completely bewildered Jack. He had expected me to come grovelling for the money and then agree to a television series as a condition of payment. At bottom it was all a big game, but I was determined not to give Jack the satisfaction of winning. There's an old Northern saying, 'There's no pockets in shrouds'. If there had been, Jack would have had an extra large pair sown into the lining. He went to the grave owing me the money.

The irony was that I had already appeared on television. In 1953 I was one of the guests on 'For Your Pleasure', a Command Performance recorded live before the young Queen Elizabeth and Prince Philip. Also in the show were Norman Wisdom and Jimmy Edwards.

I decided to do the 'golf routine', which had remained virtually unchanged since the time I performed it at St Annes in front of Julie Andrews' stepfather. The sketch was straightforward enough, but my entrance was anything but simple. In common with all the other performers I was to emerge from within the bowels of a

[93]

huge 'pie', whose crust slowly opened out for my entrance. There was a short flight of steps inside the pie and then a longer flight on the other side leading down to the audience. Over my shoulder was a bag of golf clubs which I would rest against a music stand. I suppose that if anyone should have come on from inside a pie, it was me. However, this little art director's dream quickly turned into a nightmare.

On before me was Sally Barnes, a lovely soubrette and, as I was soon to discover, an extremely athletic young girl. When she finished she trotted back up the steps and, as the pie crust creaked open, literally dived in on top of me as I stood waiting at the bottom of the steps. I collapsed in a tangle of golf clubs and flashing legs. Fortunately the audience could see none of this, but I'm sure they heard it. I shovelled the clubs back into the bag and stumbled up the steps. By now the pie crust was beginning to close down. I blundered on, and as I came into view the heavy wooden lid caught me a fearful crack on the back of the head which rang like a pistol shot across the studio. As I tottered towards the audience the only thing I knew was that I was on. The music stand loomed in front of me like a friendly landmark, only to collapse under the weight of the golf bag. It got a big laugh and is about the last thing I clearly remember about that particular performance.

After the show the entire cast were presented to the Queen and Prince Philip, who said to me,

'Did your head get a bit of a bang when you came on?' Silently I pointed to a lump the size of a duck egg swelling on my head.

'For Your Pleasure' had certainly not been for my pleasure, and I remained extremely sceptical about adapting to television. In any event, did I need it when I could pack them in at the Adelphi, as I did in my second big London run with 'Such is Life'. The show was a milestone not only for me but also for a young singer by the name of Shirley Bassey. During the run-up to the show I was approached by an agent, Michael Sullivan. He told me that he had a singer under contract, still very young, whose only experience had been in the clubs. Jack Hylton had already been introduced to her at the Albany Club and wanted her in the show. Shirley oozed star quality, but she was still very raw. In the middle of our first rehearsal the assistant stage manager Johnny Russell came up to Jack and myself looking as if he was about to press the panic button.

'This girl only knows three songs,' he told Jack, 'I Can't Give You Anything But Love, I'm Nobody's Sweetheart Now, and another one which for the life of me I can't remember at the moment.'

Jack didn't bat an eyelid. He took a few puffs on his cigar.

'Get Ross Parker to write her a song,' he finally said. Ross Parker was the man who wrote 'There'll Always Be An England' and was under exclusive contract to Hylton.

'And tell him to make it sexy,' Jack added.

'It's not enough,' continued Jimmy, 'she can't walk – she's got no idea of stage craft.'

'OK, then we'll stop her from walking, won't we Al?' Ask wardrobe to make up a gown so tight that it'll lace her knees together. And put a big flair on the bottom.'

'Well that still leaves her hands,' said Russell. 'She's equally hopeless with them.'

'Easy,' replied Jack, 'get her to stroke her tits and wave her hands about. That should just about do it.'

Thus in a few minutes in the stalls of the Adelphi the Shirley Bassey style – right down to the slinking walk and the outstretched hands – was dreamed up. Ross

Parker finished the job with a song entitled 'Who's Gonna Burn My Candle at Both Ends'. Shirley was still so innocent that she didn't fully grasp the meaning of lyrics like 'who's gonna spark my ignition, who's gonna find the key?' But the audience did. When she made her entrance down a long flight of stairs every man in the audience was drooling. With her tremendous magnetism and personality, she took that theatre over. A great star and a lovely girl – Shirley Bassey.

All the time the show was running I was keeping a close eye on the sausage business. Every day I kept office hours in my dressing room, ably abetted by my assistant Richard Lancaster. Laughter was my concern in the evening, but during the day I wrestled with the problems of sausage casings and pie fillings. Initially there had also been some problems over the translation of some of my radio material to the stage. One of my radio favourites was 'The Latecomers', in which a couple of tipsy holiday-makers – both played by Read – find themselves locked out of their boarding house. This presented me with an immediate problem – it was a long and an elaborate sketch and I could hardly play both characters myself. I needed a stooge and during rehearsals tried out Jack Tripp an excellent light comedian who was also in the show. I played the 'loudmouth' and Jack was the small nervous put-upon character. It just didn't work. Jack seemed to be aiming for some drama award and was going way over the top with the drunk bit. In a short time the entire sketch slid off balance. Jack Hylton was not entirely sympathetic when I told him how difficult I found it to work with someone else.

'You're making a big fuss over nothing,' he told me. I persisted, and suddenly he lost his temper. Purple-faced he yelled at me,

'If Jack's not good enough, we'll get somebody else! I

[96]

don't care who it is – or what it costs. You want Olivier, we'll get Olivier for you!' By now I was beginning to lose my temper too. Then my eyes fell on Richard, who had been watching the whole scene from the wings. I said to him,

'Richard, take off your glasses.' Richard was extremely shortsighted and, as everyone knows, when shortsighted people are deprived of their glasses they invariably take on a dazed and vulnerable look. It was perfect for the stooge in 'The Latecomers'. I turned to Jack,

'I'll play it off Richard, without him saying a word.'

Next day we went out together to find a costume. One of the keys to good comedy is the appearance of things being ever so slightly wrong – nothing over the top but just enough for the audience to starting working on. In a second hand clothing store we found an old dressing gown which when turned inside out and given a set of buttons, looked like the oddest overcoat ever made. In the sketch Richard came on first, clutching a big 'Police Notice' sign. He would walk centre stage before coming to a halt. Then the audience's titters were drowned by the offstage sound of the 'loudmouth' bawling out some dreadful drunken song. The routine came to an explosive climax when the 'loudmouth' stuffed a couple of bangers through the front door letterbox. At first it seems that they are duds. Then, inevitably, comes a shattering roar as they go off. Richard was magnificent. Every night for 20 minutes he maintained a perfect deadpan throughout these shenanigans. Buster Keaton could not have done better.

The show closed with a spectacular production number, 'Minstrel Melodies', along the lines of 'Showboat'. I was dressed from head to foot in white, with an enormous star-spangled topper perched on my head – not really my style at all. After a particular matinée performance I went up to one of the boxes to meet a special guest, a woman gravely ill with cancer who had been brought to see the show. I hadn't changed and was still wearing my star-spangled plantation outfit. We had a long chat and after she had left I sat for a while in the box thinking about how courageous the woman was. When I left the box I realized that the only way back to my dressing room was by cutting out of the Adelphi's side exit and nipping smartly back into the theatre foyer. I ran down the stairs and emerged in the passage which runs between the Adelphi and Wards Irish House. As the door clanged shut behind me I realized that I was not alone. Staring at this sudden apparition were two elderly Cockney women, real-life Mrs Mopps. Now this was the time of the great rock and roll explosion, and Bill Haley and his Comets were over in the country on a tour. There had been near riots wherever they had played. It seemed that the mood had also caught the two old dears in the passageway.

'Cor, oo's 'e?' One of them said with a sharp intake of breath.

'I dunno,' said her companion, 'but let's mob 'im!' I hightailed it back in to the theatre as fast as my legs would carry me.

A few days later I met some real Bill Haley fans, on stage at the Adelphi. One of my routines began, 'These days everyone's going a bit Edwardian in their dress. A pal of mine – a bus conductor – picked up a couple of Teddy Boys the other day. When they got on, he told them, "I thought you were waiting for a stagecoach." '

Mingling with the laughter was a confused roar of barracking. Beyond the lights I could see them, sitting in the stalls: six Teddy Boys, dressed to the nines in drape coats, drainpipe trousers and brothel creepers. There

[98]

was enough grease in their hair to oil a box of Home Guard rifles. They had taken my joke more than a little personally.

'We've got some trouble here,' I thought. 'How can I defuse it?' I motioned backstage for the spots to be put on them.

'We've got some friends here,' I told the audience, 'would you like to come up?' Up they came, still looking aggressive but blinking in the lights. A rustle of anticipation went round the auditorium. What would happen next?

'Now, lads,' I said pleasantly, 'what would you like to sing?' Complete collapse of Teddy Boys. They were suddenly dumbstruck.

'How about "Maybe It's Because I'm A Londoner",' I suggested. By now the flags of surrender were out. I asked the audience to give them a big hand as they went back to their seats. When I left the theatre that night, they were waiting for my autograph outside the stage door.

As you've been reading along, I expect that a small voice in the back of your mind has been asking, 'What happened to that motor car Al bought for the Command Performance?' Was I left with a white elephant? The answer, as the Americans say, is in the negative. I found a good use for it in pantomime, where I was playing Buttons in Cinderella. Driving on every night in that weird contraption made me feel more like Noddy than Buttons, but in the end the car paid its way.

Looking back, I have appeared in a dozen pantomimes – some superb, some fair to middling and some . . . well, the less said about them the better. The first came straight after the Adelphi run with 'You'll be Lucky' – Cinderella at the Empire Theatre, Liverpool. Taking on the role of Buttons was a big challenge, particularly as I have always been the world's worst at learning other people's lines. When I signed the contract I could still remember my chaotic efforts with the Water Rats all those years before. Jack Hylton remained sceptical about my chances.

'I hope you know what you've taken on,' he told me. 'You'll need some new material to play the part. You won't be able to rub along on 'The Decorator' as you've been doing at the Adelphi.' It was food for thought.

Sometimes you don't need to be clever – just lucky. One night towards the end of the Adelphi run, Bud Flanagan strolled into my dressing room.

'I hear you're going to play Buttons in Liverpool, Al. First time in panto, isn't it?'

'It certainly is,' I replied, 'I'm not sure that I'm letting myself in for.'

Then kindhearted Bud took me into his confidence.

'The great thing is, Al, to play Buttons with sympathy. Always make it sincere – he's an "everybody's mug" character, which invariably gets the laughs. But the scene to remember, and the one that really matters for you, is "The Kitchen Scene". You know, when I played Buttons at the London Coliseum, I wrote a song especially for that scene. It goes like this.' Then Bud sang it for me in his own inimitable style. It was a typical Bud Flanagan song, utterly simple but full of Bud's marvellous sincerity and in the same idiom as 'Underneath the Arches' and 'Strolling'. When he finished, Bud sat back and asked me,

'How do you like it?'

'Fabulous,' I replied.

'Well, I tell you what – I'll give it to you. I'll send you the words and the parts. If you sing it in that tempo, you'll stop the show.'

I can remember 'The Kitchen Scene' as if it was yesterday. Buttons comes into the kitchen to find Cinderella sitting there by herself, sad, forlorn and close to tears. In his naive way Buttons does his best to cheer her up.

'Now, what are you laughing at, Cinders?' Bit by bit he drags it out of her – she's not going to the ball.

'Never mind, Cinders. Come and sit up here on the table. I'll give you an orange. That'll make you feel better – a nice juicy orange. We'll put everything right. We'll think of something. How would it be if we had a "pretend ball"?'

'A "pretend ball", Buttons?'

'Yes, here in the kitchen. Why not? Now, let's see. First of all you need a fan. Wait a minute, here's one,' and Buttons hands her a frying pan. 'And a string of pearls.' Round Cinders' neck goes a long string of sausages (naturally). 'Now, we shall need a coach . . . The table. That's it. I'll be the coachman. You can imagine the horses.'

'Oh, this is wonderful, Buttons.'

Buttons edges shyly along the table towards Cinderella.

'Cinders, do you love me?'

'Well, Buttons, I do like you.'

'Only like, is that all?'

'Well, yes, Buttons.'

'Right – give me my orange back.'

This was the cue for Bud's song:

I wish Cinderella could love me.
I do, I do, I do.
And if she would think something of me
I'd never again be blue.
I wish I could be her Prince Charming,
And make her dreams come true,
I wish Cinderella could love me,
I do, I do, I do.

[101]

The last verse was sung by Buttons and Cinders together as the lights were slowly dimmed, leaving just a spot on them as they sat on the table. On the last line the light faded out altogether. Not a dry eye in the house. Thank you, Bud Flanagan, dear Bud.

That's the pantomime Cinderella we all cherish, complete with a leggy Prince Charming and a glittering coach pulled by a team of miniature ponies. At least, that's what the audience sees. Backstage, bedlam frequently reigns. The ponies may look sweet but they can be cussed little customers. It was always relatively easy to coax them down to the theatre basement to get them spruced up for the show. Persuading them to come back up again was another thing entirely. They often chose to become particularly obstinate at the precise moment that the band were striking up their entrance music. Many's the time I've come out of my dressing room to help the handlers with a strategically placed shove. Sometimes Cinderella got the same treatment as we tried to squeeze both her and her crinoline ball gown into the tiny coach. Sometimes further disasters lay in wait. On one occasion the coach rumbled on to the stage, only for the back wheels to fall off. It brought the house down.

A year later I found myself playing Wishy Washy in Aladdin. My costume was mislaid at the dry cleaners and that night I appeared in a hastily modified pair of Hardy Amies pyjamas. One Christmas, in Leicester, I was cast as the villain in Robinson Crusoe. My first entrance was through the stage trap door. The system was worked by three brawny stage hands who sweated away at a complicated tangle of ropes and pulleys which looked like a mediaeval instrument of torture. On the first night I shot up towards the stage like a bullet from a big gun. My hat fell over my eyes and I almost tripped over my big cutlass into the orchestra pit. For a moment my mind went blank, then I blurted out, 'Hello Cinders.' Momentarily, I had forgotten which pantomime I was in. There was a huge roar of laughter, and as a result I kept it in for the rest of the run. I must confess, though, I was never asked to play Robinson Crusoe again.

CHAPTER 4

The Price of Fame

CHAPTER 4

The Price of Fame

Fame has its price, its advantages and its pitfalls. Sunny uplands beckon to those able to capitalize on their success. Yawning gulfs lie in wait for the unwary.

Sometimes fame can be no help at all. On a trip to Ireland to see some two-year-olds at Ballsbridge, I found myself in friendly company in Tim Carroll's bar. At the time, in London, Danny Kaye was playing the Palladium and drawing capacity audiences. We were talking about the art of comedy, when a wizened little fellow on the edge of the group interrupted the conversation.

'I've heard of this Danny Kaye feller. An entertainer, so they say. Comedy they call it. Sure didn't he decide to go and see our own George Bernard Shaw. Full of himself he was, arriving unannounced. The house-keeper told him that Mr Shaw was having tea with

[107]

friends, but did that put him off? In he marches, as bold as brass, invites himself to tea and then proceeds to entertain everyone with his own brand of clowning. Not much was said after he left. Next morning the house-keeper showed Mr Shaw the headlines in the news-papers: 'Danny Kaye Injured in Car Crash'. And didn't GBS look up and say, "I dare say".'

Kaye was a frequent performer over here in the early fifties. One day I slipped into the Palladium to watch him rehearsing. With me was the inimitable Jimmy James, one of the nonpareils of British comedy. We stood quietly in the wings, watching Kaye at work. He was having trouble with the microphone and finally called out for a stage hand to fix it.

'Leave this to me,' whispered Jimmy as he slipped smartly on to the stage. Kaye didn't know Jimmy from Adam and waited patiently while Jimmy grappled with the mike. Within a few seconds Danny Kaye had become the unwitting stooge in a classic Jimmy James routine. All around me backstage there were snorts of stifled laughter. Puffing away on his mangled cigarette Jimmy turned to the great American star.

'I do a turn or two, you know. I can sing. Would you like to hear?' Before Danny could stop him he launched himself into a crazy medley of the American's hits. Kaye's bewilderment turned briefly into anger and into the realization that his leg was being gently pulled by a great comic.

What is a star? Jimmy James and Danny Kaye provide part of the answer. The great stars are true originals – there is no one else quite like them. Laurence Olivier once said that, to be a star, 'You have to be a bit of a bastard.' That's a bit strong – there was never a kinder man than Bud Flanagan – but you have to be pretty tough to stay at the top. And, in the final count, you must be a perfectionist. In one of my Command performances I was privileged to share the bill with Marlene Dietrich. Although she was well into her fifties, she was just about the most glamorous thing I've ever seen. The word 'star' might have been invented for her. Her attention to detail was absolute. She knew more about the lighting at the Palladium than the theatre's own technicians, the legacy of all those extraordinary films she had made in the 1930s with Josef von Sternberg. I remember someone telling me that in private life Dietrich liked nothing more than to play the part of the typical German hausfrau. Hence her remarkable survival. To live like a star, to be 'on' 100 per cent of the time, can take a terrible toll.

It can also have its faintly ludicrous side. When Jack Hylton decided to marry a young Australian beauty queen, he told me that he was determined to have no publicity. By then his first wife Ennis was dead, but there was a mistress who had had two of Jack's children. I helped him to choose a little village in Italy for the wedding, a place where nobody would know us. When we came out of the church everything had gone according to plan. There wasn't a soul to be seen in the dusty little square. Jack was crestfallen. All along he had secretly hoped that there would be rows of pressmen fighting for a vantage point when he emerged with his new bride.

Best keep your feet on the ground if you want to keep your head. The trappings of stardom can sometimes trip you up. After I became a radio 'star' I received a flood of offers to use my name on commercial products. Nowadays they call it 'marketing'. A confectioner approached me with a proposal to market a chocolate bar called 'You'll be Lucky'. Eventually we agreed on a twin bar called, inevitably, 'Lucky Double'. Inside the wrapping was a small picture of myself looking at my most businesslike. In order to produce the bars the confectioner invested in an expensive new 'enrobing' machine to apply the chocolate coating. Somehow or other the machine's name always conjured up a picture of peers of the realm lining up in the House of Lords to don their chocolate regalia.

Less successful was a plan to sell 'Right Monkey' chewing gum. My father once told me, 'You know the Ten Commandments? Well, the eleventh is "Thou Shalt Not Use Thine Own Money".' I wish I had remembered my father's words when I decided to put some of my own savings into the scheme. The first batch of samples arrived in a brightly coloured box. I was invited to sample this wonderful new product. After a minute's chewing the 'Right Monkey' gum turned to dust in my mouth. Looking back, it seems like a small comment on the fleeting nature of fame.

All the fame in the world is no guarantee against the deadly British vice – snobbery. One Sunday I drove out to the Hoylake golf club with Harry Allen. We were playing the Liverpool Empire at the time and felt that a round on the famous course would do us good. It was a busy day and there was some difficulty about paying our green fees and getting a round. The club secretary, a former military man, was most 'unhelpful', as they say. Finally he asked me if I knew any members. I glanced up at the captain's board and saw the name of George Moores whom I had known for years through my sausage business. As soon as I explained this the barriers came down. We were all but escorted to the first tee. It seems that it's all right to be a sausage baron, but in some situations it's better not to mention that you are topping the bill at the Liverpool Empire!

The greatest snobs of all are servants. One summer season when I was playing at Scarborough, I rented a house, White Lodge. With the house came Collins the butler. White Lodge was Collins' house, not mine, as he soon made clear. In no time at all Collins became one big suppressed snarl. I crept around the house hoping to avoid him. One morning some friends dropped in unexpectedly. I asked Collins to rustle up some coffee.

'I'm afraid there is no Blue Mountain, sir,' he sneered.

'Well, won't Nescafé do?'

'Nescafé, sir?' He could barely bring himself to pronounce the word, 'I will see.' As he glided off to 'his' kitchen I felt like giving him a boot up his elegant backside.

If the worst comes to the worst, a servant will attempt to elevate you to the status he feels you ought to enjoy. This is to save *him* any embarrassment. In 1957 I was invited to Pat Kirkwood's wedding reception. I had known Pat from early days in Salford. Now she was celebrating her wedding in style in the Dorchester Hotel. I arrived a little early and decided to sit for a while in the lobby and observe Pat's guests as they arrived. They were a smart crowd, all out of the top drawer. Waiting for them at the top of the stairs was a magnificently attired toastmaster who announced their names – 'the Duke and Duchess of this, the Marquis and Marchioness of that', and so on. When they had all gone in I mounted the stairs. The toastmaster leaned towards me enquiringly,

'Al Read,' I told him.

'Sir Harold Freed!' he bellowed.

I thought, 'Right flunkey!'

My life in showbusiness had the appearance of glamour, but in the fifties I often found myself yearning for the simple comforts of home. Hotels are no substitute. Scratch the surface of many a five-star hotel and you reveal the squalor underneath. Long spells of hotel life have left me with a host of memories ringing from the

[111]

exasperating to the hilarious. Even something as simple as getting breakfast can become a daunting obstacle course. During the days when there was still rationing I checked into a top-class hotel in the North. Waking up the next morning, I rang for the full breakfast. After a while a maid arrived with the information that at this hotel no hot food was served in the bedrooms. However, as a special favour 'a woman on the first floor' had kindly given up her boiled eggs for me. The next morning I decided to sally down to the restaurant. I chose that most awkward of times – five to ten. As I came through the door an officious-looking little woman hurried towards me. She looked like Arthur Askey in a wig. She had spotted an intruder – me. She addressed me with that single word in the language which can be invested with so many different meanings:

'Yes?'

'I would like breakfast.'

'Breakfast is finished.'

I gazed around at the crowded dining room. At every table people had their heads buried in their cornflakes, afraid to look up at the argument that was brewing on the threshold of the restaurant. A typical English scene.

'I'll get someone to help you,' said the guardian of the dining room. A minute later the manageress arrived.

'Can I help you?' Of course she meant precisely the opposite of what she said.

'I would like some breakfast.'

The hotel's second speak-your-weight machine replied,

'Breakfast is finished.'

I decided to inject some drama into the situation.

'Look here, I've just flown in non-stop from South Africa. It's quite monstrous that I can't have any breakfast.'

At this point Arthur Askey returned. There was a whispered conversation. Then, with a triumphant smile, the manageress turned to me:

'I'm pleased to tell you that a woman on the first floor has kindly given up her boiled eggs for you.' I still wonder who was responsible for their script.

One of the profound mysteries of life is the precise time required to boil the perfect egg. For every ten people there are ten different answers. Staying in a big hotel in Hanley, I ordered breakfast in my room. Boiled eggs. The eggs arrived but were hopelessly watery. I placed another order. The second batch was rubbery enough to survive a set or two on the centre court at Wimbledon. Undeterred, I tried again. By the time I gave up, I was surrounded by about two dozen eggs and could no longer tell which was which. Later that day, at the Three Horseshoes at Wensleydale, I told my tale of woe to a circle of friends. Within a few minutes a heated debate had blown up around the imponderable question of the boiled egg. There was only one thing for it. We all repaired to the kitchen to put the various methods which had been canvassed to the test. Stopwatches were produced and bets were laid. But despite all our best efforts, the perfect boiled egg still eluded us!

Success in showbusiness had made me 'upwardly mobile' in more senses than one. I soon found myself astride a strapping horse and part of the 'hunting set'. It was a far cry from Kipling Street, where the only horses we saw were harnessed to tradesmen's drays. It goes without saying that to hunt you have to be able to ride. While I was no Harvey Smith, I had been riding for a number of years. It all started when an osteopath, Robert Ollerenshaw, recommended that I take up riding as a corrective to the problems I inherited from my bout of sciatica. In 1954, during the run of 'You'll be Lucky', I drove out to Oxshott to meet Charlie Carter, the owner of a big riding stables and a man steeped in the lore of horse-flesh. Charlie lost no time in teaching me that horses are just like people – no two animals are the same. There are plenty of lessons to be learned from horses and applied directly to life. Never have a row with a horse when there is any danger to yourself. A rogue horse will jump through a plate glass window to get rid of you. Just get off and walk away. As my father told me when I was a lad, 'Never get into a fight unless you can win it.'

One day Charlie pointed out a big, mean-looking animal which had been brought into the stables the day before.

'He was a biter,' Charlie told me, 'but he's cured himself, with a little help from me.' I asked Charlie how. He took me round to the side of the stables, where a hedgehog skin hung from the wall. Charlie unhooked it and strapped it to his arm.

'I put this on when I went to groom him. Of course, he had to have a go at my arm, but instead he got a mouthful of prickles. He won't try that again in a hurry.' Driving home I reflected that there were one or two agents who might have benefitted from a similar course of treatment.

My arrival in the hunting world came a little later. During the Adelphi run of 'You'll be Lucky' my late-night routine was unvarying: a brisk walk back to the hotel, a light snack and then bed. On this particular night I was about to book my morning call with the head porter when I felt a hand on my shoulder. Then a deep, down-to-earth North country voice said,

'Loved the show . . . haven't laughed so much in years.' The hand and the voice belonged to a burly, open-faced man well over six feet tall.

'Now come and have a drink and meet some of my

friends. By the way, my name is Bob Hanson from . . . ever heard of Huddersfield?'

It was no use trying to explain that I was about to go to bed. Gripping me firmly by the elbow Bob manoeuvred me across the hotel lobby and into the bar, where his friends were waiting.

'Well, here he is – I've got him. I told you I would. What are you having to drink? Bring the man a triple brandy.'

I was feeling pretty tired and was quite happy to allow the conversation to flow around me until one of Bob Hanson's friends leaned towards me and asked,

'Do you hunt?'

It was John King, then a manufacturer of ball bearings and now Lord King, chairman of British Airways. It was the beginning of a firm friendship.

'No, I don't hunt,' I replied, 'but I do go out riding from time to time.' I felt that John King was weighing me up. Then he asked me to stay with him at his home at Ackworth and ride out with the Badsworth hunt.

I travelled up to Ackworth after the Adelphi run had ended and the hunting season had begun. I had gone to some trouble to kit myself out with what I considered to be the correct attire: a pair of riding breeches of a type which, it turned out, might well have done the Duke of Wellington quite nicely but were now more than a little out of date; a dark grey jacket (mercifully correct); and a pair of excruciatingly painful second-hand boots. In the outfitters they told me that they had only been worn once – I'm not surprised. I completed the outfit with a bowler hat from Locks of Bond Street. How could I fail?

Ackworth Court was a superb stone house set in magnificent grounds. From its mullioned windows you looked out on to immaculate lawns and well-tended woodlands. In the elegant panelled dining room a log fire blazed in the fireplace, a grandfather clock ticked gravely away in the corner and cut glass and silverware sparkled on the sideboard.

The meet was held on the Countess of Ross' estate. I did my best to keep up and studiously avoided any heroics. I must have passed the test because a year later I was invited to John King's home at Friar's Well, Wartnby, in Leicestershire, where he hunted with the Belvoir (pronounced beaver). I drove up with John the night before the meet.

At the crack of dawn I was woken by Field, John's valet. John was taking no chances, and Field had arrived to dress me in the approved manner. No doubt it was necessary, but what a rigmarole! It was worse than struggling into a drag outfit for a pantomime. There seemed so much of it: the buff and yellow undershirt; stockings and breeches complete with red braces and rows of buttons in mysterious places. Next came the dressing room equivalent of Bechers Brook – climbing into a pair of exquisitely crafted hunting boots. It seemed more difficult than clambering aboard a hunter. What was I supposed to do with the loops which hung from the top of each boot? With an overpowering display of tact, Field took control of the situation.

'Perhaps it would be advisable to sit down, sir, and then attempt to ease the boot on, pulling firmly on the loops.' Discreetly urged on by Field, I struggled into the boots. Now came the tying of the stock. In Field's hands it was a work of art as the silk scarf was deftly looped this way and that around my neck. The only problem was that the finished product left me nearly choking to death – red-faced and pop-eyed, like one of those clubland types exploding with outrage in a Bateman cartoon. Field stepped back, eyed me up and down and pronounced that I was finished.

So I was! I was exhausted, and I hadn't even got past the bedroom door! I emerged on to the landing and moved gingerly towards breakfast. I think I now have a fair idea of the agonies Boris Karloff must have endured when they made him up to play the Frankenstein monster. As I edged my way into the dining room my movements were about as robotic. All around me was the babble of conversation – fruity , confident voices talking loudly in a foreign language, English. I managed to catch the odd word or two:

'Diana . . . blah, blah, blah . . . disappeared completely . . . blah, blah, blah . . . awful shock . . . blah, blah, blah . . . stark naked and freezing to death . . . blah, blah, blah . . . thank God Walter had the presence of mind to call a cab . . . blah, blah, blah.'

Someone helping himself to kedgeree at the sideboard seemed to understand the drift better than I had.

'Oh, yes, I've heard the story before, but not the details!'

If you've never tried to mount a 16 hands hunter when dressed ('encased' might be a better word) in my rig-out, then you've missed nowt. Fortunately, an understanding groom gave me a hefty leg-up and off we trotted to the meet. As we proceeded to the first 'draw' John King drew up beside me.

'Oh, Read,' he said, and the rest of his words were drowned in the clatter of horses and the calling of the hounds. I did my best to read his lips as I jiggled about in the saddle, but I was equally worried that at any moment I might part company with my topper. Then another rider, Brigadier 'Tubby' Cooper, rattled up on a stock-tailed, barrel-like bay. 'Tubby' was the Field Master. John told him that I was in complete agreement with him about the 'cap fee'. Cap fee? What the hell was

[117]

all this about? What had I let myself in for? It turned out that the 'fee' was my 50 guineas hunt subscription.

For a number of years afterwards I turned out with the Belvoir as often as I could. But, at heart, I felt I was not one of them. Perhaps there is a line one cannot cross, or perhaps I lacked the determination to cross this particular line. I was unwilling to masquerade as something I was not – one of the 'toffs'. This reminds me of a story about the property developer Charles Clore, who went shooting one day with the Duke of Marlborough. When Charlie asked His Grace if he could bring his (shooting) instructor to lunch, the Duke replied,

'My God, Charles, surely you don't want the feller to teach you how to eat as well!'

It was while I was up in Leicestershire, helping to raise money for the Quorn, the local hunt, that I became embroiled in one of the most bizarre publicity stunts in my career. With me on this trip was Frank Cook, a seasoned trouper who performed a cowboy singing act. Dressed from head to foot in buckskin and armed with guitar and harmonica, Frank looked like Gene Autry's younger brother – a man more at home on the prairie than in the hunting country of Leicestershire. We had agreed to open a big jumble sale – I told a few jokes and Frank chipped in with a song. When we had finished there was an anouncement over the tannoy. The Master of the Quorn, Mr Tony Murray Smith, had put up a fine hunter – named after the hunt – for auction. All money over 100 guineas was to be donated to the hunt fund.

As I watched Quorn being led around I felt a tug at my elbow. Standing beside me was the steeplechase jockey, Tim Maloney, whose career had been cut short by injury. A colourful Irishman, and a hard drinker, Tony was a great practical joker. Digging me hard in the ribs he said,

'That's a useful sort of a horse, that Quorn.'

By now the bidding had stated and the price was moving rapidly upwards. I listened to the auctioneer – 'At 330 guineas, have you finished at 330? At 350? Have you all finished at 350? At 375 . . . 375? Sold to . . .'

'Mr Al Read!'

The voice which rang out was that of Tim Maloney. I had not been keeping an eye on him and he had been bidding for me all along.

'Right,' I thought, 'I'll get my own back on the whimsical Mr Maloney.' Quickly I formed a plan in my mind.

'You say he's a good horse, Tim?'

'Oh the very best, with a "patent safety" guarantee. Sure, your grandmother could ride him to hounds.'

'Do you think my pal Frank could ride him?' I asked, pointing out the yodelling cowboy.

'Of course.'

'I'll bet you twenty quid that Frank Cook will ride him up the steps of the town hall and right into the room where we opened the jumble sale.'

We shook hands on it and I hurried off to tell Frank. He went as white as a sheet. Despite all appearances to the contrary, he had never been on a horse in his life. In a desperate attempt to call the whole thing off he demanded that Tim provide him with an American saddle.

'No problem,' said Tim, 'we've got all sorts in Leicester.'

Frank was due to perform what increasingly looked the impossible at eight in the evening. A big crowd had gathered outside the town hall. Tim arrived looking jubilant; Frank looked green around the gills and was clutching his guitar to his bosom as if his life depended on it; the only member of the throng who seemed unaffected by the mounting excitement was Quorn. He stood quietly waiting for Frank with an aloof air and a distant look in his eye.

Frank clambered aboard without too much difficulty, gripping his guitar in one hand and the reins in the other. Then he spurred Quorn towards the steps. Now Quorn had been in the Household Cavalry, so he was as quiet and as unflustered as could be. As he trotted up the steps the crowd gave way before him. Clippety clop, clippety clop, and before he knew where he was Frank Cook was staring down at a sea of expectant faces. Like the trouper he was he immediately broke into 'I Got Rhythm', accompanying himself with guitar and harmonica. As Frank and Quorn disappeared inside the town hall the crowd went wild.

After Frank's unexpected triumph I decided to ride Quorn on stage every night in my summer show at Morecambe, but I was pre-empted by Max Bygraves, who was already doing the same thing at the Palladium. In the end I went from the sublime to the ridiculous, making my second act entrance on the back of a donkey.

At the time Tim Maloney 'acquired' Quorn for me, I had bigger problems on my mind than the upkeep of hunters. Since 1950 I had been combining two careers, those of businessman and comedian. My life was spent shuttling between Manchester and London, and in the process I was running the risk of becoming the jack of all trades and master of none. In addition, my accountant was beginning to make alarming noises about the gentlemen from the Inland Revenue. I began to consider the possibility of selling the factory.

In the event the decision was taken out of my hands, and in the most remarkable manner. It happened halfway through the run of 'Such is Life'. When I arrived at the theatre early one evening I found a note from 'Old Fred', the guardian of the stage door. Three gentlemen had called and would deem it a favour if they visit me again that evening for a 'business talk'. I was to expect them 'between houses' in my dressing room. In those days we played two shows a night, beginning at 6.15pm and 8.30pm.

Shortly before I went on for the second house the three gentleman arrived, accompanied by my accountant. They came quickly to the point. They represented a big financial group and wanted to buy the factory. Would I sell it to them lock, stock and barrel?

I tried to give myself a little room for manoeuvre. I told them that Read's was an old, established family business and that I could not rush straight into such a big decision. In fact I had already made up my mind to sell, but I decided to let them wait a little longer. I left them in the dressing room and went off to perform my first 20-minute spot in the show. As I stood in the wings waiting to go on I turned over in my mind the price I had been offered and recalled some advice my father had given me – 'If you don't know the exact figure, and you have the slightest doubt, DOUBLE IT!'

Back in the dressing room the would-be purchasers of the Read sausage empire were still waiting. Taking a leaf out of my father's book I named my price and one further condition: I would require a cheque for the full amount by the end of the week. We shook hands on the deal and a few minutes later I was back on the stage. I can't say that I had banished the deal from my mind as I stood there making the audience laugh, but that night entertaining had never seemed easier.

[121]

CHAPTER 5

Don't Fight the Monster

CHAPTER 5

Don't Fight the Monster

After my experiences in the 1954 Command show 'For Your Pleasure' I kept my distance from television. To use a rugby expression, I spent the next few years 'kicking for touch'. But it soon became clear that television was playing an increasingly important part in people's lives, and in the life of showbusiness. The one-eyed monster could not be denied for ever.

I decided to adopt a novel solution to the problem which confronted me. Before committing myself to the box in Britain, I would spend some time in the United States to see how they did things over there. Thus it was that in 1956 I found myself staying in the Beverley Hills Hotel, in Los Angeles, at the start of a Read 'fact finding tour'.

In Hollywood, television was slowly but surely

toppling cinema from its throne. The great studio empires had been broken up and the old-style movie moguls had lost their touch and their nerve. The film capital of the world was fast becoming the television capital of the world, and I was there to see it happen. I was a stranger in town, but I was soon put at my ease by the English colony. James Mason, a fellow Northerner, entertained me in the Polo Lounge and introduced me to the famous Louella Parsons, the grisly old dragon of a gossip columnist who in her heyday could make or break a star. Her inside knowledge of the seamier side of Hollywood had been helped by a shrewd marriage to one of the top Beverley Hills specialists in venereal and other related diseases. The secrets of his surgery gave Louella the edge over her arch-rival Hedda Hopper. By the mid-fifties Louella was beginning to feel the power she had exercised slipping through her talons, but she was still a force to be reckoned with. She listened to me with every indication of extreme attentiveness and then went away to write a piece about me, or rather about an English comedian called 'Hal Green'.

I also ran into Noel Coward in the Polo Lounge. He was performing his legendary one-man show on the West Coast, and I enquired how he was going down. He leaned towards me, and in that inimitably urbane voice, which rang right across the Polo Lounge, he replied,

'My dear boy, we're kicking shit out of them, as they say over here.' On the next table two blue-rinsed matrons sat as if turned to stone, their frozen Daquiris halfway to their lips. Coward gave me a broad, mischievous wink.

In no time at all I got to know some of the top American comedians. One night the hotel manager introduced me to Jonathan Winters and Bob Newhart. I'm ashamed to say that I couldn't wait to show them how funny I was.

[126]

On the spot I ran through my 'Bus Driver' routine. The cynical bus driver and his mate, the nervous young conductor, are at the bus terminus, propping up the radiator:

DRIVER: Any more tea in that pot, Tommy?
CONDUCTOR: Eh . . . no . . . come on, let's get
          back. We'll have to start picking up passen-
          gers some time.
DRIVER: What are you talking about – passengers!
          We hang on here another ten minutes then I
          don't have to stop. And while we're at it,
          watch what you're doing with that bell. You
          nearly tripped me up at that last stop with
          that old lady who ran after us with her
          basket. If I hadn't been a bit nippy with that
          third gear – she'd have been on!

Newhart was sufficiently impressed with my efforts to borrow the framework and incorporate it into his own classic 'Bus Driver' monologue. Later he also Americanized one of my favourites – 'Teaching the Wife to Drive' – into 'The Driving Instructor'. Imitation is the sincerest form of flattery. It was only then that I realized how close my humour was to the deadpan monologue style used by so many of the top Americans. In spite of its origins in the working-class life of Lancashire, it seemed to strike a chord with fellow practitioners in the United States.

On a flying visit to New York I discovered that Jack Hylton's talent spotter Bryan Michie had set up an appointment for me at the William Morris agency. It was typical of Jack, as this was precisely the one thing I had asked him *not* to do. Reluctantly I agreed to keep the appointment. At the agency we had a pleasant chat with

[127]

one of its directors, but I felt that it was going nowhere. So I volunteered a quick rendition of 'The Decorator'. It went down as well as it had six years before at the Queen's Hotel, Manchester. By the time I had finished, the small office was crammed with people who had come to listen, or 'kibbitz' aas they say in America. There was a burst of applause when I finished.

'Say, Al, we must get you on the Jack Parr show,' was the instant suggestion. It was very flattering but I decided to knock the whole thing on the head. I replied, 'I have a radio show of my own back in England, I would like Jack Parr to appear on my show!' In the subsequent consternation I slipped out of the noose.

After all these years it's amusing to reflect on the Americanization of Read. British and American styles of comedy are often so different that they fall as flat as pancakes on the wrong side of the Atlantic. Dick Shawn is a great comic, but he never came off at the Palladium. I remember going to see him on his opening night. He came out, walked up to the microphone and bellowed 'MONEY!' straight at the audience. A tidal wave of embarrassment surged around the theatre. In those days this kind of approach was just too brutal for British tastes.

Shortly after my arrival in Los Angeles I was given the run of McAdden Studios, where many of the top American situation comedy series were made. The speed and professionalism with which the programmes rolled off the production line were immensely impressive. And there also seemed to be a genuine cameraderie between the stars. One small incident has stayed in my mind to this day. I was sitting in on the recording of 'The Bob Cummings Show', a very popular series in which charming, affable Bob played a photographer whose catchphrase was 'You're Gonna Love This Picture'. Bob

n Lowndes, a contemporary
Al's from the same home town
Salford, was, like Read, an
server of every-day working-
ss life. He reproduced in
ntings what Al reproduced in
rds. Here we see the chip
op in 'Love Lane Corner' and
e of Al's favourite themes,
e Football Match'.
*th permission of the Crane
man Gallery

The irrepressible mirthmaker, the great James Keith O'Neill Edwards cracking a bottle with Al at the Queen's Hotel, Manchester. Jimmy, or 'The Professor', as he was affectionately known, was Al's first guest on 'Taking The Lid Off Life' at the Hulme Hippodrome in Manchester.

Al, while on a working cruise in the Mediterranean from which he was suddenly called back to London upon the death of Jack Hylton for a memorial show at the Theatre Royal, Drury Lane. The money raised went towards a music department in Liverpool University.

On the same cruise, with Mr Roy Ashbrook, who acted as Al's manager for the trip, Mrs Ashbrook and the Captain.

Before moving to his present home on Lord Bolton's estate in Yorkshire, Al lived in what was known as the Beverly Hills of Surrey — St George's Hill, Weybridge. On the right he is pictured with his second wife, Elizabeth.

Above Al and Elizabeth in the winner's enclosure at one of their many successful races.
Below Al's second wife, Elizabeth, from her modelling days with the Liz Allen Agency.

This portrait of Al's wife, Elizabeth, hangs today in their Yorkshire home.

Above Al and his son, Howard, who carried on the Read comic tradition
as a member of the 'Candid Camera' team.

Below Al and Elizabeth enjoy the country life at their cottage home on
Lord Bolton's estate in Yorkshire, set amid 18,000 rolling acres.
TV Times/Transworld Features

also directed the show and at this point had been completely floored by the script's requirement for the offscreen noise of tunnelling termites? What the blazes did termites sound like? Everyone on the set was scratching his head in puzzlement. Then on to the sound stage strolled the small gnome-like figure of George Burns, passing through on his way to record one of his own shows with Gracie Allen.

'Gotta problem, Bob?' he asked in that marvellous gravelly voice. Cummings explained.

'Easy – get an electric drill.'

A drill was found and plugged in. George waved it around for a few seconds to make his point and then padded off, still puffing away at his big cigar, leaving Bob Cummings with his new-found sound effect. In an English studio this might have provoked a union walk-out, but at McAdden it was all part of a day's work.

During my stay in Hollywood I was able to follow the production of several of Bob's shows from start to finish. At the weekend there would be a canter through the script around the pool. On Monday everyone's movements were blocked out on the set. On Tuesday there was an informal run through in the studio, with no reference to the script, so that everything stayed loose and relaxed. By Wednesday the show was settling down into shape. Filming – on two cameras only – began on Thursday. By Friday evening the half-hour segment was cut and in the can and ready to run before a Saturday-night preview audience. The audience of about 150 was just the size to produce the right amount of laughter on the soundtrack. The whole process was smoothness itself, right down to the smartly uniformed 'greeters' who made the audience feel at home before the show was run. The cast were impeccable, embracing the camera as if it was the most natural thing in the world to do. One day George Burns gave the most succinct piece of advice I ever received about television technique.

'Don't fight the monster, Al, make it work for you.' I was to remember these words when I came to grips with TV on this side of the Atlantic.

One of the interesting sidelights on my stay in Hollywood was my introduction to the often bizarre world of Beverly Hills showbusiness life. I remember going to a birthday party at which the singer Billy Daniels gave his wife a pink Cadillac wrapped in red ribbons. Shortly afterwards Bryan Michie forwarded a script to me. It had been going the rounds, and he thought it might be just the thing to tempt me into my screen debut. The plot revolved around the adventures of an English gun salesman trying to sell his wares in the Wild West. I read through the script, which was extremely amusing, but decided that I'd better tackle the small screen before venturing on to the big one. Ironically, the film was made in Spain as 'The Sheriff of Fractured Jaw', with Kenneth More in the title role. The director was Raoul Walsh, who handled such classics as High Sierra and White Heat. The leading lady was Jayne Mansfield, which might have made it an interesting experience.

On another occasion a flashily dressed character turned up at the hotel and introduced himself as my agent. This was news to me, and I suspected another devious Jack Hylton manoeuvre. I suggested we go to Romanoff's restaurant to discuss this intriguing development. As we settled down over cocktails I asked my 'agent' what he had fixed up for me.

'Well, nothing as yet, Al. But there's one thing which we ought to discuss and that's my fee.' It was clear that his fee was about the only thing my agent was likely to fix up.

'Well it can't be too high, old man,' I replied, 'as I don't have an agent!' I let him pay for the lunch.

Eventually the time came to put my American experience to the test in British television. I had continued to hold out against all the pressure, but by the early sixties I could resist no longer. A persuasive influence was exercised by Ronnie Taylor, who had successfully made the transition from radio to television and was an associate producer on 'Candid Camera'. I was finally pushed over the edge by Richard Armitage, a young impressario who had come to see me while I was performing in a summer show at Scarborough. Richard was a new kind of impressario, Cambridge-educated and the friend of an ambitious young man called David Frost. Richard didn't smoke a fat cigar or seem to need all the other familiar props of the more traditional type of showbiz entrepreneur. I agreed to record a TV show at the ABC studios at Didsbury, on the outskirts of Manchester. Over ten years had gone by since 'The Decorator' had sent me on my way at the Queen's Hotel.

I found myself in a strange and threatening world. From day one I felt the control I had always enjoyed beginning to slip through my fingers. The irony was that although I was recycling my radio material for the television, I was completely in Ronnie's hands. He was the professional in this medium. In a sense we had, for the moment, ceased to be collaborators. Accompanied by Ronnie, I turned up at the studios for rehearsal. We walked into what seemed like a huge aircraft hanger with an endless expanse of blue-painted floor. All around me carpenters were hammering away at sets and electricians swarming over scaffolding. I felt rather small. In front of us a huge row of plaster pillars was raising itself skywards. It was as if someone had just dumped the Parthenon in Didsbury.

'Whose set is that?' I asked.

'It's yours,' replied Ronnie.

My heart sank. No one had consulted me about this monstrosity and I was at a loss as to what it had to do with 'pictures from life'. 'Pictures from Ancient Greek Life' perhaps, but a million miles away from 'The Decorator'. I began to think that television was fine, as you weren't on it.

Now came the tug of war with the camera. Facing the glass eye was a greater ordeal than the Opera House, Belfast. At least I could see the audience there. On stage or at the Paris Pullman I felt an instant and close rapport with the people I was entertaining. The television camera placed a barrier between us. Instinctively, I felt a desire to push it aside. Laughter must be shared and, try as I might, I found that I was no longer sharing it with my new audience.

Everyone realized that I felt uneasy with the camera. But the more they tried to help, the more self-conscious I felt. It was an entirely new experience. The other problem was presented by the medium itself. The medium may be the message, but this particular medium was not helping Read to get his message across. Television is a literal medium – you get what you see, no more and no less. Everyone knows the disappointment they sometimes feel when they watch the serialization of a favourite novel. The actors never seem to resemble the pictures of the characters which you have built up in your mind's eye. Anyone who listened to my radio shows could imagine for himself just what the 'loudmouth' looked like. I provided the framework and the rest was up to the listeners. In a sense they became collaborators in my comedy. But on television there is little or no room for suggestion. If you had asked ten shoppers in the high street to describe the big, menacing dog which growled its way through so many of my sketches, you would have got ten different breeds or types of mongrel. But when it came to performing the routine on television, a real dog had to be found. The country was scoured, auditions were held and the producer agonized over the choice. On the radio a strategically timed woof was enough to paint a picture of the cur having a go at the hapless postman. Both parts, of course, played by Read. On television we performed in a realistic set and with the lucky winner of the dog auditions. The paws of the wretched animal had to be taped to the top of the garden gate, while it received instructions from an off-camera handler. I stood on the sidelines shaking my head in disbelief.

It was a far cry from the early days, when Jack Hylton had said to me, 'Just go on and tell 'em.' Would that it had been possible on television! But I soon found myself in a cul-de-sac similar to the one devised by Barker Andrews in the disastrous radio 'pilot' of 1950. I was surrounded by a small army of people, all of whom had to justify their existence by interfering with my progress on to the screen.

Looking back, the most successful TV show was the first in a series for ATV produced by Leslie Chatfield. In this show at least we did not stray far from the radio format. There was very little dressing up on my part and a minimum of complicated sets. I hoped to continue the series in the same vein, but at the dreaded script conference I was overruled. The big corporate machine had taken over and I was helpless in its grip. It reminded me of the old hunter's tale: 'I've caught me a bear, and it won't let me go.'

Rehearsals for the ATV shows were at Elstree. I asked Leslie Chatfield to let me rehearse with the cameras. Perhaps this might help me to overcome my block. I was told that the cameras were needed elsewhere. Not until the day of the show would I find myself fixed in their unblinking gaze.

Nevertheless, Leslie was determined to help me.

'I'll be the camera,' he told me, and in the same breath sent out for a couple of pails and two mops. The scene I had wanted to rehearse was the 'Policeman' sketch in which the loudmouth played a cynical veteran copper and the nervous character was a raw recruit.

Early hours of the morning . . . Young recruit being taught the ropes. Insistant blasts on a Police whistle attract the attention of the veteran Copper who arrives, of breath, to discover that it is the recruit who is the cause of the whistling . . .
COPPER: Was that you blowin' your whistle Alf?
RECRUIT: Ay, I thought I saw something.
COPPER: Well, you could have looked the other way. First job to learn – never blow your whistle. You've fetched me out of a very warm shop doorway and I've spilled half a flask of hot tea all down my tunic . . . Remember – never blow your whistle . . .

When they arrived, the mops were stuck in the pails, with a property department helmet on one, representing the loudmouth, and a flat cap on the other for the recruit. Chatfield stood directly in front of me, and the two pails were placed to his right and left at an angle of 45 degrees Leslie was pretending to be the middle camera of three. This one would record my 'bridges' while the other two would record the loudmouth and recruit parts.

'Right, let's go,' said Leslie encouragingly, staring straight at me in his best imitation of an ATV camera. I began. Then, with a superb sense of timing, both the mops slowly toppled sideways on to the floor. On reflection, this might have been funnier had we kept it in the show. Leslie and I battled on for about an hour, at the end of which I was beginning to feel much more confident. Then we broke for lunch. When we returned chaos seemed to have broken out. The studio floor was covered with strips of tape, supposedly marking all my movements. Amidst all the to-ing and fro-ing I was ignored. When I resumed my unconventional form of rehearsal there were constant interruptions as I was politely but firmly moved from one mark to another. It was as if I was an inanimate object. Slowly the familiar lines began to slip from my mind. I called for the script. The words danced before my eyes. Separated from the context in which I had originally written them – the radio – they had suddenly become meaningless.

I'm not sure how we got through that series, but we did. As I became increasingly demoralized my old problem over remembering the lines returned with a vengeance. Eventually a technician suggested equipping me with a small radio receiver, inserted in my ear like a deaf aid, through which I could be fed my lines. I struggled through four shows without resorting to the fiendish device, but after this I admitted defeat and agreed to be wired up with the 'Deaf Aid' prompter. The results were novel, to say the least. The prompts always arrived fractionally after I had 'dried', making me seem like a delayed-action mechnical doll as I delivered my lines. In the heat and glare of the lights, with thick make-up plastered all over my face and the wire from the prompter running down my back, I felt more than a little inhibited.

You might expect that this marked the end of my television career. In fact, it was merely the beginning. They kept plugging away with me, and in the end I was a kind of success, in spite of the best efforts of all my helpers.

Others took to the television with the greatest of ease, not least among them my eldest son Howard. I had sent Howard to public school, so that he could acquire some of the 'polish' which had failed to rub off on me during my brief stay at North Manchester Preparatory Grammar. In the process Howard became an expert snooker player – good enough to wipe the floor with his father – but his academic record was somewhat less than brilliant. When he was 16 I decided to give him a start in the hotel business, as a trainee at the Leofric in Coventry.

Howard's headmaster was none too pleased:

'We normally keep the boys here until they are 18, Mr Read,' he told me. I thought, 'They can keep him here till he's 80 for all the difference it'll make. The lad's learning nowt.' Working in the hotel allowed Howard to give free rein to his own instincts as a performer. Like father, like son. No waiter was ever more discreetly attentive to the elderly inhabitants of the afternoon tea room. No barman ever wielded a cocktail shaker with such panache. When he was promoted to work on the reception desk no one could match the grave decorum with which he greeted the guests. They were all real 'performances', worthy of applause.

Eventually Howard's talents carried him all the way to 'Candid Camera', where he became one of Jonathan Routh's assistants and took part in many of the crazy incidents staged by the programme's young team. In one of them he pretended to be an Arab sheikh, offering a bewildered taxi driver a sliver from a huge gold bar in lieu of cash after being dropped off at the Dorchester. Howard was a born prankster, and at my suggestion he pulled a fast one on John King during a luncheon at the Mirabelle. For the part Howard transformed himself into a German. His hair was closely cropped and dyed blonde by my Jermyn Street barber. When he marched over to our table, as stiff as a ramrod, he looked every inch a Prussian officer. For a few moments we talked in cod German while my guests rose halfway out of their chairs, as Englishmen do when confronted with a foreigner. They were completely taken in. Then I turned to them and said,

'Gentlemen, may I introduce my young son Howard.' John King was delighted with the deception and immediately asked Howard to stay. Very sensibly Howard told him that he had an urgent appointment bade us all goodbye and left. Always quit while you're ahead. Shortly afterwards John King offered Howard an excellent job in one of his American subsidiaries and Howard went off to live in the United States, where he has now made his home.

One of the most significant television figures of the early 1960s was David Frost, the man who, as a wag acidly remarked, 'rose without trace'. David was an enormous success not because he was particularly funny, but because he was ambitious, shrewd and the man in the right place at the right time. My time had come in 1950. Now, ten years later, it was the turn of David and his fellow 'Footlights' satirists.

At Richard Armitage's prompting I included David on the bottom of the bill in a summer touring show. In the middle of the bill was Jimmy Clitheroe, making it one of the more unusual line-ups of the period. We opened at the Odeon Cinema, Weston-super-Mare, a big art deco monster better suited to screening 'Gone With the Wind' or 'Spartacus' than providing a showcase for variety. It was David's blooding in showbusiness proper and he was as positive then as he is now. He rushed about all over the place, referring to everything as 'Super' and displaying not the smallest sign of nerves. One day his parents turned up to watch their famous son rehearse. They seemed a bit bewildered by the whole affair.

I'm sure that David viewed everything as a grand undergraduate romp. On the day we opened he burst into my suite at the Grand Atlantic Hotel clutching a red plastic football. He looked like an excited little boy.

'Come on, Al, let's go down to the beach and hoof this around for a bit!' So down to the beach we went, Frostie, Clitheroe and myself, and on to that enormous expanse of sand – the walrus, the carpenter and their eager young assistant chasing after a plastic football. By the time we arrived at the theatre David was in a state of euphoria which bordered on the hysterical. He was jumping about in his dressing room, apparently brimming over with confidence. Nevertheless, he was still very much the beginner and I had to help him with his make-up. He ended up looking as if he was auditioning for the part of the Last of the Mohicans, but it just about passed muster. Then the great moment arrived. On he bounded to the strains of the signature tune of That Was the Week That Was. He died the death. Clearly there were very few satire lovers taking their holidays in Weston-super-Mare that week. There was hardly a laugh. But to David it was just water off a duck's back. Springheeled as ever he bounced off, scattering fusillades of 'Supers' about him as he rushed back to his dressing room. What a tour! But, in the end, I had to hand it to David, who was determination personified. We have remained good friends ever since.

There was one transition which I found much easier to make than that from radio to television. In the late sixties I took my act on to the northern club circuit. Not the old-style working-men's clubs of my youth but the brash, glittering fun palaces which had mushroomed in the affluent sixties. No performer was too big for them. A host of top-line Americans were winging their way across the Atlantic to perform at clubs like The Talk of the North and Newcastle's Dolce Vita. Read took the road north in his Rolls.

The Dolce Vita had made me 'an offer I couldn't refuse'. I set out for the north-east wondering what awaited me there. I need not have worried. I received the warmest of welcomes and the coldest of champagne in my dressing room. I felt instantly at home. I had given a great deal of thought to coping with the demands of playing a big club. Holding the audience's attention from the moment you walk on is absolutely crucial. All around people are eating, drinking and talking; if you don't grab them straight away, you're lost. To make sure that I did, I got my chauffeur to build me a small wooden platform covered in dark black material. My plan was to walk straight on as the lights went down and mount the platform as a couple of spots swung straight on me. By now everybody's attention should be focussed on me. The scheme worked perfectly, and I used it in all my subsequent club performances.

The Talk of the North, in Eccles, was a favourite venue. After two successful dates there I felt that I had to come up with 'something completely different', as the Monty Python team used to say. I decided to resurrect 'The Latecomers'. My son Alexander knocked up an impressionistic set and volunteered to play the policeman who comes in at the end of the sketch. My second wife Elizabeth played the floozie who distracts the tipsy revellers. And a young friend of Alex stepped into the shoes so ably filled at the Adelphi by Richard Lancaster. So far so good. However, there was one outstanding problem. At the Adelphi we had used a 'bomb tank' to contain the thunderflashes which were detonated as the bangers exploded behind the boarding house door. Alex suggested that we substitute a dustbin. During rehearsals we set the dustbin up at the side of the stage and primed it with the thunderflashes. When the moment came they went off with a shattering roar and clouds of evil-smelling smoke. When it cleared the dustbin lid had disappeared. I noticed Alex pointing excitedly upwards and as my gaze followed his arm I saw the lid embedded in the ceiling. Like naughty children who have just broken the next door neighbour's window, we decided to scarper before the club's owner arrived. That night the sketch went ahead without the explosion. Needless to say the audience were fascinated by the sight of a dustbin lid seemingly suspended over their heads. After the show, the owner came into my dressing room.

'You know, Al,' he said, 'it's the damndest thing, but we've got a dustbin lid in the ceiling. For the life of me, I can't think how it got there. I'm amazed you didn't notice it during your act!'

CHAPTER 6

Elizabeth

CHAPTER 6

Elizabeth

Marriage is often the victim claimed by a life in show-business. Long periods of separation can act as a solvent on even the closest of relationships. During 1954 I hardly spent a day at home. Joyce and the children had to come to see me, which was no substitute for home life. Travelling took its toll: trips to America, summer shows, recording dates in London, all of them forced Joyce and myself farther apart. It was clear that our marriage had come to an end. The separation was amicable – Joyce was and is the warmest and most level-headed person I know – but there was now nothing I could do to reverse the process.

Then I met Elizabeth. It was in 1959, and once again I was staying at the Mayfair Hotel. Late one morning, as I strolled through the lobby with Richard Lancaster, my attention was captured by the young woman standing behind the counter which sold theatre tickets to the hotel's guests. Tall, blonde and cool, she was a stunner. She stopped me in my tracks.

As I stood there, momentarily transfixed, she gathered up her things and handed over charge of the desk to a colleague. Perhaps she was going out for a lunchbreak. It seems absurd now, but at that precise moment I couldn't bear the thought of her disappearing through the hotel's swing doors. Impulsively I walked over to her, introduced myself and enquired whether she would like a lift in the car which was waiting for me outside.

I was in a daze as I opened the car door for her. We drove off to Regent Street, where she intended to buy some shoes. By now I was completely captivated. I dismissed the driver, forgot all about my lunch appointment and I helped her choose a pair. My offer to pay for them was politely declined. There was something about this young woman's elegance and meticulousness which I found irresistible. As we left the shoe shop I asked her to dine with me that night.

We went to Jack Isow's, a Jewish restaurant in the West End patronized by theatre people. On the backs of the plush leather seats were emblazoned the names of the showbusiness and sporting personalities who had sat there. Jack Isow was a benevolent-looking, tubby little man – a kosher Friar Tuck – but there was steel underneath the surface. Albert Dimes, the old gangland boss, was one of his associates, and Jack could take care of himself. But running right through him was a wide sentimental streak. I remember him telling me that his pride and joy had been a pet budgie which would perch on his chest when he was in the bath. One day the little bird flew out of the open bathroom window and was never seen again. 'It broke my heart, Al,' Jack told me.

Elizabeth was entranced by Jack Isow's and shortly afterwards I invited her to one of the parties I threw there from time to time. Among the regular guests were Sir Bernard and Lady Docker, whom I had known for years. Nowadays the mention of Norah Docker is sufficient to raise a cynical smile. But in the austerity years after the war, when the Dockers were at the height of their fame, their extravagant antics provided the public with a great deal of harmless amusement. I say 'their' antics, but really I mean Norah's. She never let up. Life for her was a constant exercise in controlled exhibitionism and vulgarity. Gallons of pink champagne and gold-plated Daimlers were only the tip of the iceberg. One of my parties ended with Norah challenging all the men to a game of marbles. There she was on the floor in her expensive evening dress, scrabbling away with the best of them. Naturally she won (she was actually Women's World Marbles Champion in 1955). Standing diffidently on the fringe of things was poor old Sir Bernard, looking as if he could never quite grasp what had hit him. Norah had filleted him, and now she just had him in tow.

Not long after meeting Elizabeth I travelled north to Manchester for a Christmas show at the Opera House in which Dora Bryan played alongside me. Dicky Hurren was the producer, a tremendous martinet but a superb professional. When he told me that the show was to be called 'Words and Music' I pointed out that Noel Coward had got there first. 'Sod Noel Coward!' Dicky said, and on we went.

One of the routines I had planned for the show was the 'Car Park' sketch, in which I played a cantankerous attendant who emerges from a scruffy little cabin on the side of the stage. Dicky wanted to switch the cabin from one side of the stage to the other, a move which would

[145]

have thrown the whole routine out of joint. He was always more concerned with the overall mechanics of the entire show than the preferences of individual artists. I objected. There was a brief exchange which Dicky brought sharply to an end.

'Strike the set!' he shouted, 'the Car Park is out. Al will do "The Latecomers".' Then he turned on his heel and stalked off. It was decisive, to say the least, but he was right.

Sets proved particularly troublesome during that show. In one of my sketches with Dora we played a couple of Lancashire lasses on holiday at Blackpool. Ronnie and I had worked it up years before and, rather unkindly perhaps, always referred to it as the 'Tarts Sketch'. It was another 'picture from life' – two girls out for a good time, hoping to get their hands on a nice feller. However, Dicky Hurren's mania for spectacle rather got in the way of this basically simple idea. There was a swimming pool, filled to the top with water, into which – you've guessed it – we were both meant to take a tumble at the end of the sketch. On the first night we both went in, with a tremendous splash. There was water everywhere. That was the last night Dora went in. I was left to take a ducking twice nightly. As I towelled myself down in the dressing room every night I thought, 'Surely we could manage without this.'

It was during this show that I learnt that Elizabeth had been seriously ill with jaundice. When she was ready to convalesce I invited her up to stay in Manchester. Rest and fresh air were what was required, and every day we drove out into the beautiful Cheshire countryside. By now we were fast becoming inseparable and Howard was affectionately referring to Elizabeth as 'The Princess'. But problems remained. I was still married to Joyce and Elizabeth was separated from her husband after a brief, unhappy first marriage.

Moreover, Elizabeth's extended stay in Manchester meant that she had to resign from her job at the Mayfair. When she was fully recovered, she returned to London to work for Jaeger. Then she was offered the opportunity to go to Nassau, in the Bahamas, where Jaeger were opening a new branch. I urged her to take the job, telling her that it was the opportunity of a lifetime. I saw her off at Heathrow as she boarded one of those massive old turboprop airliners to New York. She was carrying with her a small Teddy Bear I had given her that morning. Teddy is still with us.

Elizabeth quickly settled down in Nassau, moving from Jaeger to a small, exclusive boutique called Ambrosine's. I took every opportunity I could to see her, and for two years virtually became a citizen of the Bahamas. I rented an appartment on Cable Beach, with a vast picture window in the sitting room which looked out on to the sea, and settled down to observe the life of the super-rich.

People used to say of the Bahamas that there was enough money on the islands to sink them. There was no shortage of fat cats whose business was only 51 per cent legitimate. But no one asked too many questions. Underneath the glittering surface scandal lurked, like so many time bombs waiting quietly to go off. In July and August the rains came in Nassau. Water cascaded through the streets and rats paddled along on the breast of the tide. That was the other side to Nassau, the side that the tourists never saw.

It was inevitable that in Nassau I should run across Norah Docker. Out in the bay her huge yacht Shamara rode at anchor. I was invited to lunch at twelve o'clock the following day. As I rode out to the yacht in the launch I glanced at my watch and noticed that I was a bit late. I thought no more about it until we drew up alongside. I could see Norah pacing the quarterdeck in a towering rage. Blackbeard himself would have stood no chance against her in that mood. I never got on board. She leaned over the side and subjected me to a tongue-lashing which could have been heard back on the quay and no doubt for several miles inland. It would have brought a blush to the cheeks of even the most hardened sergeant major. I chugged back to the quay with 'Get back to ******* Blackpool!' ringing in my ears.

Norah was always completely unpredictable. Several years later I bumped into her in a smart restaurant in Switzerland. Norah swarmed over to my table, the incident in Nassau obviously completely forgotten. After exchanging a few words she jumped to her feet and marched over to the small stage where a band was playing. Grabbing the microphone, she announced, 'Ladies and Gentlemen, tonight we are privileged to have with us that great comedian Al Read. Come on up, Al, and entertain us.' I was squirming with embarrassment, but when Norah's imperious hand was extended you did not refuse – not if you knew Norah. Of course most of the diners in the restaurant were Swiss or German and didn't have a clue who I was. So much for changing the potential of comedy throughout the world! So I busked it, getting the band to accompany me on the Maurice Chevalier imitation which I had performed years before at Bolton. Then, mightily relieved, I crept back to my seat.

The last time I saw Norah was at the St Brennard's Hotel in Jersey. There they both were in the corner of the restaurant, looking a little elderly now. Sir Bernard seemed more like a moth-eaten Saint Bernard than ever, but Norah was still at it, knocking back the pink champagne and generally dominating the proceedings. I quietly slipped away, leaving Lady Docker to the other diners, the band and – fourteen years later – a rather sad and lonely death in the Great Western Hotel, Paddington.

Nassau had more than its share of beautiful women but there was none lovelier than Elizabeth. I was not the only one to think so, however. One day, while I was staying at the Dorchester, I received a telegram: UNOFFICIALLY ENGAGED, LIZ. That was it. No details. I didn't have to think twice. Within hours I was on the first available plane to New York. There was absolutely no way that I was prepared to accept this without a fight. Unofficially engaged? Not bloody likely!

I checked in at the Emerald Beach Hotel and met Elizabeth. Who was her 'unofficial fiancé? She told me that she knew very little about him except that he was a South American and a champion ballroom dancer. The Cesar Romero type. Apart from that he was a mystery man.

I found out his name, and bright and early the next morning I paid a call at the hotel where he was staying. I got his room number from reception and rang him on the inhouse telephone.

'I know your name but I don't think you know mine,' I told him. 'I'm not sure what your intentions are with Elizabeth, but there's no doubt about mine. I'll tell you who I am when I see you down here in 15 minutes time.'

He was down in five minutes and we were facing each other in reception. Did we have a fight? No, we had breakfast! I told Roberto a few things and found out plenty. The following morning he left the hotel and has never been heard of since.

After two years in Nassau, Elizabeth decided to fly to New York in a bid to achieve a long-cherished ambition. She gave herself three weeks to break into the world of modelling. She started from scratch, with no friends or contacts in the fashion business. Her first move was to look through the Yellow Pages. She picked out the Cy Perkins agency. At her interview she was signed up, but was given strict instructions to shed 20 pounds before her first assignment, which was an advertisement for Drambuie liqueur. Soon she was flying to and fro across the States promoting the drink. I came out to see her as often as I could, staying at the Drake or the Plaza; in the summer months, when New York becomes a gigantic Turkish bath, Liz flew over to England to see me in my summer shows in Blackpool, Morecambe and Scarborough. In fact there was a great deal of to-ing and fro-ing during that period in our lives. Joyce decided to move to Philadelphia, where Howard was working, and settle down there.

By 1965 Elizabeth was eager to return to England. I had bought a house on Saint George's Hill, Weybridge, set in three acres of grounds, in anticipation of our eventual marriage. Everything seemed set, but once again Liz grew restless. While I was working on a new television series she flew back to New York. The next thing I heard was that she had been seen on the arm of Eddy Low, an immensely wealthy toy manufacturer.

Once again I found myself flying across the Atlantic, this time to head off the determined Eddy Low at the pass. When I saw Elizabeth again she had a big engagement ring on her finger. It looked as if she had made up her mind to stay in America.

I decided to see Joyce in Phildelphia and travelled down on the train. It was wintertime, the snow lay deep on the ground and it was bitterly cold. I don't think that I have ever felt so low in my life. As I watched the bleak countryside flashing past, my father's words raced through my mind: 'If you think you're defeated, you are.'

When homely, comfortable Joyce answered the door

her first words were, 'Have you had your tea?' It was like being back in Lancashire.

'You'll stay the night won't you?' asked Joyce. I needed no persuasion, and after dinner I poured out my heart to her. She listened intently and when I had finished she said,

'I might have met someone else too.' And indeed she had, a man by the name of Reed! She had fallen in love with him and they wanted to get married. The next morning she rang Eddy Low in New York and explained the whole situation to him. She was filing for divorce, which would leave me free to marry Elizabeth. As always Joyce was calm, sensible and matter-of-fact. It probably saved the situation.

Then, at Joyce's suggestion, I travelled back to New York to see Elizabeth. We met in the lobby of the Drake – two people in the big city. By now we had both made up our minds. There was to be no turning back. Elizabeth put her hand in mine, and it has been there ever since.

But there were still the formalities to go through. We were all to fly to Juarez, in Mexico, to obtain the divorce. Elizabeth and I decided to stay on there to get married. First we had to clear up Elizabeth's affairs in New York. Then we were delayed by bad weather. Waiting in the stuffy bedroom of the airport hotel I flicked on the television. By some strange twist of fate I had turned in to the screening of 'A Taste of Honey', filmed in the streets of my home town of Salford and starring Rita Tushingham and my old friend Dora Bryan. It was a poignant reminder of where everything had started.

In Juarez the temperature was in the nineties. At the civil wedding ceremony I slipped a thin band of gold on Elizabeth's finger. It had cost only a few dollars, but it meant more to us than a crate of Cartier's diamonds. Life seemed at its sweetest. Back at the charming old hotel we danced the night away underneath a lush canopy of bougainvillea. I felt the loudmouth leaning over my shoulder and telling me, 'You'll Be Lucky'. But he didn't know just how lucky I was.

After our marriage Elizabeth and I moved into a beautiful house on St George's Hill in Weybridge. This was in the days before the area had been colonised by showbusiness people. The three acres of grounds were lovingly tended by a crotchety gardener who would not allow Elizabeth to pick the daffodils. I mean *his* daffodils. He was the horticultural equivalent of the butler at Scarborough.

It had always been an ambition of mine to live in Weybridge, but somehow I felt cut off from my roots there. Comfortable though life was, it seemed a little too neat and manicured. A bit too Southern for my tastes, perhaps. We decided to move back up North.

When I was still a lad I remember pestering my father to buy a billiard table. His reply was characteristically down to earth: 'Go and play on someone else's – that way it'll cost you nowt.' When we left Weybridge for our new home I took my father at his word. I had often pictured myself living on a country estate, but the trappings of the gentleman farmer seldom come cheap. So, in my father's words, I decided to 'play on someone else's estate.' Lord Bolton's to be precise, 18,000 rolling acres of it in the beautiful Yorkshire countryside. Elizabeth and I acquired a charming old lodge on the edge of the estate which to this day remains our home in England.

I also built a house in Spain, near Almeria, and in the 1970s Elizabeth began to spend more and more time there. After recording four radio shows for the BBC in 1976 – the only ones that now survive in their archives – we became almost permanent residents in Spain.

[152]

After a while I began to realize that one can have too much relaxation. Life was sweet, the sea sparkled and glinted away as we sat on the terrace, and the local people were friendliness itself. But there was something missing. You can be a star for so long that you take all the attention for granted. I had come to Spain for peace and seclusion, but these were now beginning to pall. Ironically it was a situation reminiscent of Jack Hylton's wedding in Italy: the elaborate plans for maintaining secrecy and then the all-too-clear disappointment when the photographers failed to show up. One day, on a visit to London a women came up to me in Harrods and asked, 'Weren't you Al Read?' She had a point.

Then I received a telegram from the BBC. 'By 'eck, are they still in business then?' I asked Elizabeth when she brought it out to the terrace. It appeared that Aunti Beeb wanted me to get in touch right away, with a view to guesting on the Michael Parkinson show.

My first inclination was to say No. I had only appeared once before on a chat show, and that had been back in 1963 in America with Johnny Carson. It had not been the smoothest of rides. Before the show Johnny and I had carefully run over the questions that he was going to ask me. But as soon as I settled down in the interviewee's chair and the applause had died down Johnny launched into a completely different line of questioning to the one we had planned. I virtually dried up! Moreover, Parkinson was television, and the bug-eyed monster had already caused me enough headaches. Once bitten twice shy.

I declined, but the BBC persisted. Another telegram arrived almost begging me to change my mind. I spoke to the show's producer, John Fisher, on the phone and he told me that by hook or by crook he was going to get Read on the show. Eventually I relented, but with one

[153]

condition. I wanted to top the bill. Now this was at a time when Parkinson's guests were, almost without exception, the heavyweights of the entertainment world: John Wayne, Gregory Peck, Sophia Loren – you name 'em and Parky had gazed adoringly at them over his famous clipboard. This presented John Fisher with a small problem. He wrote back to me asking what would happen if, on the evening I appeared, Barbara Streisand and Frank Sinatra also turned up. Tongue only slightly in cheek I replied that in such a situation Frank and Barbara would have to stand down! In the end it turned out that Roger Moore was the other main guest that night, and James Bond graciously conceded star billing to The Decorator.

Several weeks after tying all the arrangements together Elizabeth and I arrived in London for my final confrontation with the television camera. As I walked down the flight of stairs towards Parkinson, with the band playing 'Such is Life', George Burns' words went through my mind: 'Don't fight the monster – make it work for you.'

For a few brief seconds it looked as if my encounter with Parky might turn into a Johnny Carson Mark 2. He had given me a fantastic build-up before I came on, and the applause had been more generous than I could have hoped for in my wildest dreams. Then came the first question which, I must confess, I had written myself.

'I believe your father was a sausage maker.' This was going from the sublime to the ridiculous, but that's what good comedy is all about.

'That's right, Michael,' I replied, 'in fact I come from a long line of sausages!'

There was a big laugh, and for the first time on television I began to relax. I wasn't doing one of my routines straight to camera, I was simply chatting away to Michael and letting it all flow naturally. All those years

[154]

before, Jack Hylton had urged me, 'Just walk on and tell 'em.' Now I was doing just that.

In no time at all I found myself explaining the roots of my comedy and how it sprang from the gossip I heard all around me in Salford when I was a lad. The tittle tattle that makes the world of ordinary folk go round; the exchange of rumours and confidences in small confined places – in the corner shop, on the top of the bus. Almost without thinking I moved into improvising a sketch on the spot – two old biddies gossiping about Margaret Thatcher: 'Of course, we knew her father, Alf. Used to keep a corner shop, you know. Had pigeons at the back too. You had to be careful when you went out to the you-know-what at the bottom of the garden – if you pulled the wrong chain, you let the pigeons out!'

Then Michael said to me, 'Surely, Al, there's one thing you just can't do on television – your dog'.

Without pausing I replied, 'As a matter of fact, Michael, I've got him with me here tonight. He's locked away safely in the dressing room. No, I tell a lie – his handler's brought him into the studio.' Then I turned to address an imaginary group of people off camera – 'Don't let go of him . . . grrrrrrr . . . No, no, drop that cable . . . grrrr grrrr . . . Drop it, drooooop it! . . . wooof, woooof!'

I could see the dog there, *and so could the audience*. I had made him REAL – more real than the wretched mutts we used in the television shows. Somehow I had created a little bit of radio on the television. But more than that I had finally made the monster work for me. It had taken a long time, but it was worth it.

Well, that's it. The evening is drawing in as I lay down my pen for the last time. I hope you've enjoyed reading the book as much as I've enjoyed recalling my life. Outside in the gathering Yorkshire dusk I can see a young lad trotting down the road back to a warm winter fire. A scruffy little fellow, with his head packed full of dreams, no doubt, just as I was at his age. I have been so lucky, as most of those dreams have come true. The headlines read 'From Sausages to Stardom', but these words can't do justice to the happiness and heartaches which lay along the way. But then, 'Such is Life!'

INDEX

ABC studios, Didsbury, 131
Ackworth Court, 115
Adam, Ken, 67
Aladdin (pantomime), 102
Albany Club, 87
Allen, Fred, 66
Allen, Gracie, 32, 129
Allen, Harry, 44, 82, 85, 110
Almeira, Spain, 152–3
Alport (naturalized German), 21
Andrews, Barker, 61–2, 66, 133
Andrews, Julie, 57
Andrews, Ted, 57, 93
Armitage, Richard, 131, 137
Ashbrook, Roy, 37–8
Askey, Arthur, 66, 87, 92
ATV company, 133–4

Badsworth hunt, 115
Bahamas, 147–9
Barber's shop' monologue, 68–9
Barnes, Sally, 94
Bassey, Shirley, 95–6
Belfast Opera House, 44
Belvoir hunt, 116–18
Bennett (driver), 25–6
'Birth of the New Baby, The' (sketch), 91
'Black Velvet' (show), 48
Black, Alfred, 84
Black, George, 35–6, 48, 87
Black, Pauline, 36
Blackburn: Theatre Royal, 29
Blackpool, 40–2, 79
Bluett, Kitty, 56
Bolton: Grand Theatre, 44–6
Bolton, Lord, 152
Brandon, Johnny, 80
Bristol: Hippodrome, 88
British Broadcasting Corporation (BBC),
    11–12, 61–7, 73, 82, 152; see also
    individual programmes
Bryan, Dora, 145–6, 151
Buchanan, Jack, 92
Burden, Albert, 42
Burns, George, 32, 129–30, 154
'Bus Driver' (routine), 127
Bygraves, Max, 120

'Candid Camera' (TV series), 131, 136

'Car Park' (sketch), 145–6
Carroll, Tim, 107
Carson, Johnny, 153–4
Carter, Charlie, 114
Cave, Paul, 65
Chatfield, Leslie, 133–5
Chatham: Theatre Royal, 48–9
Cinderella (pantomime), 99–102
Clapham: Grand Theatre, 49
Clarke, Alfred, 31
Clitheroe, Jimmy, 36, 91, 137–8
Clore, Charles, 118
Collins (butler), 110–11
Cook, Frank, 118–20
Cooper, Brigadier 'Tubby', 117
Coward, Noel, 126, 145
Cross, Robin, 68
Cummings, Bob, 128–9

Daily Mail Radio Awards, 74
Dalziel, May, 55
Daniels, Billy, 130
Dawson, Les, 71
'Decorator, The' (routine), 61–3, 78, 82,
    100, 128, 131–2
Dietrich, Marlene, 109
Dimes, Albert, 144
Docker, Sir Bernard, 145, 148
Docker, Norah, Lady, 145, 147–9
Donegan, Lonnie, 83
Dors, Diana, 84

Eccles: The Talk of the North club, 139
Edmonds, Sam, 23–4
Edwards, Jimmy, 92–3
Edwards, Percy, 72
Elizabeth II, Queen, 93–4
Elizabeth the Queen Mother, 91–2
Elstree, 133
Entwhistle, Fred, 32
Evans, Norman, 71

Faulkner, Max, 31
Field (valet), 116
Field, Sid, 35–6, 81, 83
Fisher, John, 153
Flanagan, Bud, 100, 102, 108
Florrie, Aunty, 42
'For Your Pleasure' (TV show), 93–4, 125

[157]

Francis, Douggie, 46
Frax Fratters (canned meal), 40
Frost, David, 131, 137–8

'Gardener, The' (routine), 78–9
George VI, King, 78
Glendenning, Raymond, 44–5
Gordon, Noele, 48
gossip, 69–71
Greenwood, Walter, 17, 87
Grocer's Society, 31

Haley, Bill, 98
Hall, Henry, 66, 79–81
Handley, Tommy, 66
Hanson, Bob, 115
Hay, Will, 29
Hayes, Pat, 67
Henry, Charlie, 90
Henshall, William, 35
Hill, Ada, 44
Hill, Joe, 44–5
Holloway, Stanley, 31
Hollywood, USA, 125–6, 129–30
Home Guard, 38–9
Hopper, Hedda, 126
Hoylake golf club, 110
Hudson, Sergeant (Home Guard), 39
Hughes, David, 80
Hurren, Dicky, 145–6
Hurricane, HMS, 38
Hylton, Ennis (Jack's wife), 109
Hylton, Jack: eats pie at Ascot, 29; puts
  AR in Adelphi show, 84; as agent,
  86–7; tricks AR, 87–8; and set for AR
  show, 91; owes money to AR, 91, 93;
  and TV, 92–3; and Shirley Bassey, 95;
  and AR's stage partner, 96–7; and AR
  in panto, 100; remarries, 109, 153; and
  AR in USA, 127, 130; and AR's TV
  appearances, 155

innuendo, 70–1
Isow, Jack (restauranteur), 144–5
'It's That Man Again' (ITMA; radio
  show), 66

Jackley, Phil, 49–51
James, Jimmy, 108
Jaye, Bobby, 12
Jewel, Jimmy, 56
Jolson, Al, 45
'Joys of Motoring, The' (sketch), 89
Juarez, Mexico, 151

Karloff, Boris, 117
Kaye, Danny, 107–8
Keaton, Buster, 97
Keel, Howard, 83
Kilburn Empire, 30
King, John (later Lord), 115–17, 136–7
Kirkwood, Pat, 111
Knight, Dame Laura, 36
Kordites, the (group), 64
Korris, Harry, 83

Lancaster, Richard, 96–7, 139, 143
'Latecomers, The' (routine), 96–7, 139,
  146
Leigh, Piers, 76, 78
Levene, Harry, 47
Liverpool: Empire Theatre, 110
Logan, Jimmy, 55
London: Adelphi Theatre, 84, 86, 93–4,
  98–100, 114, 139; Coliseum Theatre,
  74–5; Mayfair Hotel, 85, 89, 143;
  Palladium theatre, 89, 107–9; Paris
  Pullman cinema, 71
Loren, Sophia, 154
Los Angeles, 125, 128
Low, Eddy, 150
Lowndes, Alan, 18
Loy, Myrna, 32
Lytham St Annes, 57, 58

McAdden Studios, Los Angeles, 128–9
Madison Square Gardens, New York, 47
Maloney, Tim, 118–20
Manchester: Opera House, 145; Palace
  Theatre, 47, 91; Queen's Hotel, 58
Marlborough, Duke of, 118
Martin, Ray, and orchestra, 67
Mason, James, 126
Michie, Bryan, 127, 130
Midland Towers holiday camp, 41
Miller, Max, 49
Modley, Albert, 92
Moore, Roger, 154
More, Kenneth, 130
'Morning After the Night Before, The'
  (routine), 75
Morris, Dave, 82
Morris, William (agency), 127
Moss Bros. (outfitters), 76–7
Moxon, Billy, 90–1
Murdoch, Richard, 66
Murray Smith, Tony, 118
Musical Elliotts, 49

NAAFI, 36, 80
Nassau, Bahamas, 147–9
Newcastle on Tyne: Dolce Vita club, 139
Newhart, Bob, 126–7
New York, 47, 127–8, 149, 151; *see also* United States of America
'Night Out With the Boys, A' (routine), 75
North Manchester Preparatory Grammar School, 25, 136
Nottingham, 80–1, 85

Olivier, Laurence, 108
Ollerenshaw, Robert, 113
'Over to You' (show), 48–51, 56, 85
Oxford: New Theatre, 87

pantomine, 99–103
Parker, Ross, 95–6
Parkinson, Michael, 73, 153–4
Parnell, Val, 82, 89–90
Parr, Jack, 128
Parsons, Louella, 126
Peck, Gregory, 154
Peers, Donald, 72, 76
Percy, Billy, 41
Perkins, Cy (New York agency), 150
Petulengro, Madame, 80
Philadelphia, 150
Philip, Prince, Duke of Edinburgh, 93–4
Piddock, Barry, 48–51
'Policeman' (sketch), 134
Powell, William, 32
Pringle, Harry, 49

Quorn hunt, 118
Quorn (horse), 118–20

radio, 61–7, 73, 82, 92
Randle, Frank, 44, 83–4
Rawicz and Landauer (pianists), 72–3
Ray, Ted, 47–8, 50, 56
'Ray's A Laugh' (radio show), 56
Read, Al: birth and early home life, 17–20; schooling 20–1, 25, 136; success as salesman for family business, 25–7; at soccer matches, 27–8; early theatre-going, 29–30; works in family business, 30, 46, 53, 58, 73, 84, 96; monologues, 31; golf, 31, 82, 110; first marriage, 32; wins wartime meat contract, 36–7, 80; in Home Guard, 38–9; sciatica, 39, 113; first engagements, 41–2, 44–6; prosecuted

for Sunday performances, 42–3; buys car, 45; boxing promotion, 47; loses money in backing show, 48–51; declines TV audition, 57; radio acts, 61–7, 73, 82; on comedy, 67–72, 128, 155; wins Daily Mail award, 74–5; entertains royal family, 76–8, 91; stage performances, 79–81, 84–5; fortune told, 80; and 'silken cord', 86; acquires horses, 88–9, 120; Royal Command performances, 89–90; buys stage car, 89–91, 99; TV performances, 92–4, 125, 130–6, 154; in pantomime, 99–103; on stars and stardom, 107–9; advertising, 109–10; on snobbery, 110–13; horse-riding and hunting, 113–20; sells family business, 120–1; in USA, 125–31; uses 'deaf-aid' prompter, 135; tours northern clubs, 138–40; divorce and second marriage, 143–4, 151; houses, 150, 152; *see also* individual shows and sketches
Read, Alexander (son), 139–40
Read, Bill (brother), 37
Read, Edward (Ted; uncle), 21–3
Read, Elizabeth (second wife): and AR's BBC invitation, 11; as critic, 32; plays in AR sketch, 139; courtship and marriage, 143–7, 149–51; jaundice, 146; works in Bahamas, 147–149; modelling in New York, 149–51
Read, George (uncle), 21–3
Read, Herbert Henry (father), 21–4, 46, 56, 66, 71, 110
Read, Howard (son), 136–7, 146, 150
Read, Joyce (first wife; *née* Entwhistle), 32, 59, 143, 146, 150–1
Reddington (*later* Felton), Tommy, 47
Rediffusion (company), 92
Reindeer, Eddie, 48
Revnell, Ethel, 45–6
'Right monkey' (catch phrase), 73
'Right Monkey' (show), 80–1
Robinson Crusoe (pantomime), 102–3
Ross, Annie (Annabelle), 55–6
Routh, Jonathan, 136
Royal Command Performances, 83, 89–91, 125
Russell, Johnny, 91, 95

St George's Hill, Weybridge, 150, 152
St John's Infants School, Salford, 20
Salford, 17–18, 155
Sanders, Doug, 31

Scarborough, 110–11
Shaw, George Bernard, 74, 107–8
Shawn, Dick, 128
'Sheriff of Fractured Jaw, The' (film), 130
Short, Jack, 55
Sinclair, Peter, 77
Slaughter, Tod, 29
Smythe, Monty, 88–9
Solomons, Jack, 47
Spain, 152–3
Sternberg, Josef von, 109
'Such is Life' (signature tune and radio
    show), 64
'Such is Life' (Adelphi show), 93, 95–7,
    120
'Such is Life' (racehorse), 88
Sullivan, Michael, 95
Sunday Observance Act, 42

'Taking the Lid off Life' (radio show), 67
'Tarts Sketch', 146
'Taste of Honey, A' (film), 151
Taylor, Bill, 91
Taylor, Jack, 41–2
Taylor, Ronnie: collaborates with AR,
    62–8, 73, 146; and Donald Peers, 72;
    auditions comedians, 74; helps AR
    with motor car, 90; TV work, 131–2
'Teaching the Wife to Drive' (routine),
    127
television, 57, 92–3, 125, 130–6, 153
Television Wales and the West (TWW),
    93
Thatcher, Margaret, 155
Thomas, Terry, 78
Thomson, Roy, 2nd Baron, 92

Tiller girls, 84
Tripp, Jack, 96
Tushingham, Rita, 151

United States of America, 125–31; see also
    New York

'Variety Fanfare' (radio show), 61–3, 65,
    72–3, 92
Vickers, Gilbert, 22
Vickers, Hedley, 21–2, 36
Vickers, Lawrence, 22

Walker's (Bolton grocer), 26
Walsh, Raoul, 130
Wardle's (Manchester pie-shop), 28
Warris, Ben, 56, 58
Water Rats, 58, 100
Watts, Michael, 13
Wayne, John, 154
Webster, Peter, 40–1
West, Gracie, 45
Weston-super-Mare: Odeon Cinema,
    137–8
Weybridge, 150, 152
Wilkinson's (Farnworth grocer), 25–6,
    37, 65
Windsor Castle, 76–8
Winnick, Margot, 77
Winters, Jonathan, 126
Wisdom, Norman, 93

'You'll be lucky' (catch phrase), 19, 49, 73
'You'll Be Lucky' (show), 42, 99, 113–14
'You'll be lucky' (racehorse), 88–9